CW01497725

Rebellion Against Henry VIII

Rebellion Against Henry VIII

The Rise and Fall of a Dynasty

Phil Carradice

First published in Great Britain in 2022 by
Pen & Sword History
An imprint of
Pen & Sword Books Ltd
Yorkshire – Philadelphia

ISBN 978 1 39907 176 5

Typeset by Mac Style
Printed in the UK by CPI Group (UK) Ltd, Croydon, CR0 4YY.

Pen & Sword Books Limited incorporates the imprints of Atlas,
Archaeology, Aviation, Discovery, Family History, Fiction, History,
Maritime, Military, Military Classics, Politics, Select, Transport,
True Crime, Air World, Frontline Publishing, Leo Cooper, Remember
When, Seaforth Publishing, The Praetorian Press, Wharncliffe
Local History, Wharncliffe Transport, Wharncliffe True Crime
and White Owl.

For a complete list of Pen & Sword titles please contact

PEN & SWORD BOOKS LIMITED
47 Church Street, Barnsley, South Yorkshire, S70 2AS, England
E-mail: enquiries@pen-and-sword.co.uk
Website: www.pen-and-sword.co.uk

Or

PEN AND SWORD BOOKS
1950 Lawrence Rd, Havertown, PA 19083, USA
E-mail: Uspen-and-sword@casematepublishers.com
Website: www.penandswordbooks.com

Contents

Introduction

Any assessment of the reigns of kings and queens during the medieval period will quickly show that in almost every instance, periods of confusion and trouble outnumbered those of calm. Peace and harmony were rare commodities.

Even the most beloved of sovereigns faced moments of disorder and disruption at some stage in their periods on the throne. How they responded to those periods is what made them great or weak monarchs. More importantly, it is what continues to make their reigns fascinating for historians and storytellers. In this, King Henry VIII, arguably England's most famous – or infamous – ruler was no different from the rest.

Although discontent during Henry's reign did sometimes morph into unrest or riot, unhappiness was equally as often manifested simply in grumblings and mutterings in the bar room or on the village green. It was only when such grumblings became the substance of complaints from those with money and power to do something tangible about them, that discontent moved into the more dangerous area of disorder.

Disorder and disturbance to the people, to the economy of the country and to life in general in the kingdom of England and Wales during the reign of Henry took several different forms. Some were dangerous and life-threatening, others were merely annoyances that still needed to be dealt with either by the nobles or by the king.

The obvious disturbance came in the form of rebellion, an upsurge of emotion and power designed to discomfort or even displace the king. The Pilgrimage of Grace of 1536 was the most significant uprising of the sixteenth century, not just for Henry himself but for any of the great Tudor monarchs.

As the rebellion swelled and grew in strength it seemed for a brief moment as if the uprising was powerful enough to threaten the stability of Henry's entire regime. The 'Pilgrimage' – surely a misnomer as far as its name was concerned? – seemed to be saying that the King's 'Reformation' of the Catholic Church in Britain and the destruction of the monasteries had been a step too far.

However, 'the Pilgrimage' was not the only expression of discontent aimed at Henry VIII and his regime. There were several other rebellions, armed uprisings that required the urgent attention of the king and his ministers. Most of them needed to be put down by the force of arms, some at a local level, others on a national scale.

During Henry's reign, there were also a long and regular series of riots, mainly in the rural areas of the country. Usually, such riots were concerned with such things as poor harvests, the lurking threat of rural famine or the imposition of enclosures on common land. Some of these revolts were more significant than others but virtually all of them were dealt with at a local level.

Then there was war. War brought the king considerable glory – glory that he had dreamed about nearly all his life. Even before he became king martial glory was always one of his main aims particularly when it was combined with spectacular events like the famous Field of Cloth of Gold.

Henry quickly learned that fighting a war on the continent of Europe also brought problems and difficulties at home, problems such as he had never dreamed about. In 1513 it brought a full-scale invasion by the Scots, an event which took place at the most inopportune moment in the whole reign. The invasion could easily have resulted in Henry's still-brittle edifice crashing down around his ears.

The matter of Henry's divorce and the subsequent break with Rome led to more discontent than anything the country had ever seen, including the recent Wars of the Roses. Quite apart from being the main cause of The Pilgrimage of Grace, the emotional and spiritual upheaval that the schism caused to thousands of ordinary citizens is hard to assimilate or assess. Suffice to say its effects were still being felt hundreds of years later.

Perhaps the most unusual and most unexpected disturbance to the lives of people in sixteenth-century Britain came from the repeated outbreaks of what became known as the sweating sickness. This plague-like epidemic hit the country on at least five separate occasions from 1485 onwards, causing hundreds of deaths and spreading wide-ranging fear and disruption in all sections of society.

The cause of the disease was unexplained, many seeing it as God's punishment for such things as the dismembering of the monasteries and the break with Rome. Even now its origins remain unclear but at the time it caused panic across the whole country.

Henry VIII made sure that he slept in different beds every night while the disease was rampant, hoping against hope that it would keep away. He might have escaped the ravages of the sweating sickness, thousands did not. Even Cardinal Wolsey in his elegant palace of Hampton Court was afflicted with the sweating sickness on two separate occasions.

Henry's character was such that he could never accept any blame for the troubles that assailed his kingdom, troubles large and troubles small. As a consequence, his chief advisors, men like Bishop Richard Foxe, Cardinal Wolsey, Sir Thomas More and Thomas Cromwell were the ones who shouldered much of the blame when things did not go quite the way the king wanted. Most of them suffered the ultimate punishment for their failures.

Success, when it came, was considered Henry's prerogative and was rarely attributed to his ministers or advisors. Regardless of success or failure, Wolsey and the others were the men who did their best to make the king's bidding a reality and must, therefore, be an integral part of this book.

The reign of Henry VIII, a relatively short period of just thirty-nine years, began with joyous celebration at the arrival of a shining new king and ended with widespread terror at the rantings of a psychotic overlord. There is enough disturbance and disorder there to last for a dozen lifetimes. Much of that disorder Henry brought on himself.

Rebellion, disturbance and disorder. They may have created turbulence in the lives of Tudor men and women but they also made for one of the most fascinating reigns in English history.

NB

While I have attempted to maintain a broadly chronological approach to the subject it has not been possible to stick rigidly to such a style. The incidents of riot, rebellion, disorder and disturbance are the key elements of the story told here. They did not occur in an orderly fashion and while, in the main, I have followed a logical pattern there are certain incidents that have had to be taken out of time and context. Hopefully that will add to rather than distract from the reader's enjoyment.

Chapter One

The King is Dead, Long Live the King

Henry VII, first of the Tudor monarchs, died at 11.00pm on Saturday 21 April 1509. Despite being wasted by tuberculosis – after the Black Death and the Sweating Sickness perhaps the most dreaded and incurable disease of the day – he died relatively peacefully at the elegant and luxurious Richmond Palace which he had built for himself on the banks of the River Thames. He died believing to the last that he had done his duty and made England and Wales a safer place for his subjects.

Henry's demise, in bed 'with his boots off' so to speak, was in contrast to so many of his predecessors who had ended their lives on the battlefield or in mysterious and unexplained circumstances in dark and dank fortress dungeons. He had survived plot and counter-plot and had suffered more than enough in his role as king. He was content now to join his beloved wife Elizabeth and his recently deceased son Arthur in the Paradise he was sure was waiting for him.

Regardless of his painful illness, Henry passed on to the next world having made his peace with God. He died surrounded by his servants and chief advisors, clutching in his hand the traditional lighted taper to illuminate his way into the arms of his maker.

Henry Tudor had seized power in 1485, defeating and deposing King Richard III at the Battle of Bosworth Field. He had not been expected to win the battle but thanks mainly to supreme acts of treachery by some of Richard's most senior officers, Henry emerged victorious. He subsequently ruled England for twenty-four significant years, not necessarily a long reign but one which had been emotionally and physically demanding.

Usurper he may have been but Henry's actions effectively ended the chaos of the Wars of the Roses and at his death, he handed over the dynasty and leadership of the country to his only surviving son. That son, Henry VIII, became the first monarch for nearly two centuries to succeed to the throne of England without the very real threat of death and destruction hovering over his shoulder.

Or maybe not. Even as he waited anxiously to take possession of the crown Prince Henry's position was far from safe. As soon as he ascended the throne, the seventeen-year-old king was in a more perilous position than he had ever been at any stage in his life. Inevitably, with all of the arrogance of youth, he did not seem to realise the precariousness of his position!

On the surface, he was confident, self-important and full of bluster. In reality, however, the new king was vulnerable and wide open to mistakes. He did not even know where he could place his trust or with whom to share his innermost fears. The Tudors had not been in control long enough for the succession to take place seamlessly and effortlessly and that made the bough on which young King Henry was balancing a very delicate and flimsy perch indeed.

Prince Henry was the younger son of Henry Tudor and had not expected to become king, not until his elder brother Arthur died suddenly, without warning, in April 1502. The next seven years had been a period of rapid learning for the prince but, even so, by 1509 he was still far from ready to assume the reins of power. In particular, the in-fighting and Machiavellian intrigues of court life made him susceptible to strongly voiced opinions from men who were supposedly there to guide and advise him in his new role.

Obviously, over the next thirty years, the personality and character of Henry VIII developed and changed. One constant remained, however. Throughout his turbulent life, he continued to be highly susceptible to the opinions of others. It lasted and defined him even as he began the slow slide from uncertainty into the depths of paranoia.

Arguably, Henry was fortunate in that he had a wide range of individuals to advise him. Cardinal Wolsey, Thomas Cromwell, the radical thinker Dr William Butts, even the court jester Will Sommers all influenced his life and his political decisions in one way or another. Sommers, in particular, became almost a constant companion in the final fraught years of Henry's life. There were those who thought taking advice from a fool to be typical of the king but many of his advisors, official and otherwise, had their own agendas and it is unlikely that Henry could have done without any of his inner circle.

The writer and chronicler Polydore Vergil summed up the situation when he wrote about the relationship between Henry and the much-maligned Cardinal Wolsey:

> He (Wolsey) would inculcate, instil and drum into his ears that the commonwealth was in a bad state because of its many governors, since each one was serving his own interests. But if the supreme administration of affairs were entrusted to himself, undoubtedly he would deal much better with public affairs without bothering his prince.[1]

It was a somewhat partisan view, written later in Henry's reign and presented with Vergil's tongue pressed firmly in his cheek. Yet Wolsey's willingness to shoulder the burden of state affairs fitted easily with Henry's overriding love of life. The king's concentration span was short; he was always prone to making sweeping judgements and the minutiae of business usually failed to impress him for longer than was absolutely necessary.

There is, therefore, more than a grain of truth in Vergil's comment and it was not long before Wolsey had gained almost complete control over his king. That was a situation that would last for nearly twenty years. As Vergil went on to write 'Henry considered everything just and right that was suggested to him by Wolsey'.[2]

It was not just Wolsey. There were many more who strove to influence the king. Some like his early advisor Richard Foxe were successful, others simply fell by the wayside. And it had all begun with the situation he had 'inherited' on becoming heir apparent to the English crown.

In many ways, Henry's adolescence, lodged as it was in the final years of his father's reign, had been a difficult period. It was a time when uncertainty and fear of what might happen in the future appeared to consume the kingdom. With everyone dreading a return to the Wars of the Roses, they were dark and dangerous days.

Henry was given little, if any, instruction on how to conduct himself as the king he would become and he was certainly awarded no responsibilities or duties to help prepare him for the role. He would have loved a better, more in-depth relationship with his father but that was not to be. Instead, there was almost a feeling of resentment from Henry VII who perhaps saw in the young man many of the qualities he would have liked to possess himself.

Henry VII had been devastated by the death of Arthur, his beloved elder son and, not long after that dramatic event, he was further shattered by the demise of his wife. The marriage between Henry and Elizabeth of York had been a political one but, amazingly, the two lynchpins of the Lancastrian and Yorkist lines fell deeply in love with each other, so much so that their marriage became one of the great royal love affairs.

Elizabeth's death in 1503 left the King bereft of comfort and solace. It took several weeks before he was able to emerge from self-imposed isolation and he was never quite the same man again. All that now remained for him was to ensure the security of his line and, through the continuation of his dynasty, the safety of the country. To achieve that end the monarchy needed to be financially secure with the result that those final years of Henry's reign were marked by the emergence of two significant factions within the royal court.

At one extreme, at the end of a long list of advisors, stood the members of the Privy Council. They were the traditional coterie of courtiers and royal officials who had been advising the sovereign for decades. At the other pole or extremis lurked a darkly sardonic and menacing pair of lawyers, Richard Empson and Edmund Dudley. They were new to the game of royal diplomacy but were adapting and gaining power much quicker than anyone could have ever dreamed possible.

Amongst Henry VII's earliest advisers had been men like Thomas Howard (Earl of Surrey and later Duke of Norfolk), John Morton, inventor of the infamous Morton's Fork and the Archbishop of Canterbury William Warham. Morton died before the first Tudor king, Warham not long after, but while they were alive and fighting on Henry's behalf, they were important figures in the country.

As far as Henry was concerned the biggest advantage of these men was that they were, in the case of Surrey/Norfolk, already part of the very rich nobility of the country. As far as the other two were concerned, they were individuals who could be rewarded for their service by being promoted within the church for which they supposedly worked. Both options were something that cost the crown absolutely nothing. And that pleased Henry, always shrewd or careful with money.

On the other hand, Empson and Dudley were different. They did not come from any of the great families of the country and they were most certainly not working members of the church.

The two lawyers were self-made men. Their success – and therefore the king's – depended on their ability to carry out the wishes of the monarch. Their reward would come in their appointments as nominated officers of the crown, in the influence they could wield and in whatever extra-curricular activities they could devise.

As the dying king rasped out his final few breaths, the minds of those who clustered around his bed – almost all of them his long-time supporters and comrades – were racing. They were intent not only with finding ways to keep the new monarch safe but with plans and schemes to ensure their own security, wealth and positions of power.

The first important step was perhaps the most difficult. Disposing of potential threats like Empson and Dudley had been on all their minds for years but the way to do that was not yet clear to everyone – apart perhaps from one man, the redoubtable Bishop Foxe. More of him later.

A new king was a vulnerable king, particularly one as young and inexperienced as Prince Henry. Whatever people had felt about his father, it was obvious that the old monarch had at least provided a degree of security for his people. Pretenders to the crown, men like Lambert Simnel, Perkin Warbeck, even the hapless Earl of Warwick, had all been dealt with. They had been defeated in battle and sent to the Tower, humiliated in the public stocks or, if necessary, executed.

As for the ordinary people, the traders and farmers, the shopkeepers, clerks and clergymen of England, the coming of the Tudors meant there was no looting or wholesale destruction of their property as there had been during the Wars of the Roses. For most of Henry Tudor's reign, the populace lived in a relatively safe environment where security and prosperity were, before long, taken for granted.

Arguably, Henry had never been in serious danger of losing his throne. Apart from there being a distinct lack of credible alternatives, any invasion or uprising would have required enough support to make it acceptable to the masses. For those who were that way inclined, it was important to ensure that an uprising did not appear to be 'a self-interested act of political speculation either by foreign powers or by isolated English malcontents'.[3] Perkin Warbeck was probably the one pretender to best fit the bill but most of the other examples of discontent were minor in the extreme.

In the main, the remaining members of the defeated House of York had simply buried their heads to await a more opportune moment to rise up and once more push their claims for power. Buried heads there might have been but the ailing Henry and his advisors knew that the Yorkist threat had not gone away. Members of the House of York could easily renew their claims and activities, particularly in uncertain times such as the accession of the new king.

Nearly all of the king's advisors were men who had experienced the ravages of the Wars of the Roses when for thirty blood-soaked years the two Royal Houses of York and Lancaster had flung themselves at each other's throats. None of them wanted a return to the brutality of such a destructive and damaging civil war.

Most prominent amongst those gathered around the death bed of the king was Richard Foxe. Accurately named, as Bishop of Winchester and Lord Privy Seal he had been at the centre of Henry's government for years. He was, amongst other things, spymaster general and was the man who happily masterminded many of the king's more successful policies both at home and abroad.

Over the last few years, however, Foxe had watched helplessly as the two hated hatchet men of the king, Richard Empson and Edmund Dudley, had grown steadily in strength and power. Together, the pair had risen in status until their position seemed to be virtually unchallengeable.

Now, the physical decline and death of the king had placed into the hands of Foxe a way of dealing with these dangerous and despised opponents. At the same time, he saw an opportunity to secure the new monarch on the throne. It was an aim that was not totally altruistic as ensuring young Henry's safety would also ensure Foxe's own continued standing and position.

At the time of Henry VII's death, Empson and Dudley were perhaps the most reviled men in England. Hated by the nobles, despised by the courtiers, feared by the emerging monied classes, their reputation spread much further. Implausible as it might seem, by 1509 the mere mention of their names was enough to cause dread and terror in the minds of even the lowliest peasants in the land, men and women who were really beneath the radar of Empson and Dudley:

The pair ... by every means fair or foul vied with each other in extorting money. Whomsoever, whether nobleman or man of the people, their informers charged with the flimsiest or vaguest false accusations, Empson and Dudley condemned and deprived of their property. They proceeded against not the poor but the wealthy, churchmen, rich magnates, even the intimates of the King himself.[4]

The two men worked independently, Empson as Chancellor of the Duchy of Lancaster, Dudley as President of the King's Council. Their aim, however, was the same – to raise money for the Crown. They ruthlessly increased taxes and rents, seized land and property, controlled customs duties and sold offices to the highest bidders. In less than four years Dudley alone had raised over £200,000 for the king, a sum in the region of nearly a million pounds in today's money!

Both Empson and Dudley sat as prime movers on *The Council Learned in the Law*, a small and compact legal body created by Henry and used in conjunction with the *Court of Star Chamber* to keep the wealthier and more truculent noblemen of the country in line.

The Council was particularly active in prosecuting nobles accused of keeping retainers. Retainers or private armies were a definite 'no-no' in Henry Tudor's Britain where ownership of a personal troop of soldiers was considered just one step away from open rebellion. The king's rationale was simple – if you have a private army, it will not be long before you start to wage a public war.

Guilty men were hauled before *The Council* or *Star Chamber* and given a choice – pay a fine now or go to court where the punishment will be considerably greater. Most nobles were taken aback by the 'invitation' to cough up there and then but after a little reflection soon saw sense in the option. It was little more than state-controlled bribery but those who had been caught out invariably cursed their luck, surrendered their retainers and paid their slightly lower fine to the king and to *The Council*. Much the best result all round!

Less dangerous but equally as unsavoury crimes were also dealt with by *The Council*. The Earl of Northumberland, for example, was once fined £10,000 for ravishing one of the king's wards. He was obliged to make a down payment of £5,000 and the rest was held against him to ensure good behaviour in the future.[5]

Neither Empson nor Dudley was above resorting to violence, often having the king's debtors beaten if they did not comply with their wishes. On a whim, or if they felt there was no other way, they had men thrown into prison to await trial where 'stacked' juries would return the verdict wanted by the king. It was, in many respects, a reign of terror:

> Daily in the halls of Empson and Dudley's houses (were) a host of persons awaiting sentence, to whom wretchedly evasive replies were given, so that they were exhausted by the duration of their anxiety and voluntarily gave up their money, rather than remain longer in that sort of agony ...The most savage harshness was made complete.[6]

It was brutal and it was punitive and yet the two tax gatherers had done only what Henry VII had wanted and expected of them. With the king's approval, their clutching hands had reached out to encircle anyone whose fortunes might be better employed by being distributed a little more liberally! If there was money floating around – anyone's money – then it would do better by being diverted into the pockets and purses of the Tudors, the king's in particular.

At the same time, it was, of course, inevitable that some of the readjusted and realigned finances also managed to find their way into the hands of Messrs Empson and Dudley. It was almost expected in the pre-civil service world of Tudor England and both men became inordinately wealthy. The richer they grew the more powerful they became.

It had been a swift but seemingly unstoppable rise to the top for Empson and Dudley as they ruthlessly raised taxes, enforced enclosures of common lands and manipulated penal laws in favour of the crown. They lived in style, Dudley purloining houses and land in sixteen different English counties and shires. Richard Empson acquired huge estates in counties like Gloucestershire and Oxford. He also made himself a considerable fortune by gaining control of a large number of lucrative wardships.

Their main duty, however, was to the king and by the final year of his life, true to their charge, Empson and Dudley had made Henry VII a very rich man. In doing so the pair had become far closer and more indispensable to the king than Bishop Foxe had either expected or wanted. He had been powerless to prevent it and was forced to bite his lip and await his moment. In the meantime, hatred and envy of Empson and Dudley continued to grow.

The two tax gatherers were aware of the rancour attached to their names but dismissed it simply as the emotions of the masses. They still felt totally secure, knowing they had the backing of the king, particularly now when he was growing older, more infirm and less able to do the job himself. Put simply, they knew Henry VII could not do without them.

However, the king's final illness could not have come at a better time for the members of the Privy Council. Men such as Foxe, along with old comrades like Sir Thomas Lovell and the newly arrived and hugely ambitious Thomas Wolsey, were born opportunists, happy to seize their chances as they came. And now, fate, in the form of the longevity of mankind, had placed them in a position where they could not only rid themselves of Empson and Dudley but also guide the new, impressionable monarch along the route they wanted him to take.

Foxe and the others were well aware of the power which rested with Empson and Dudley. They knew that the deadly duo presented as much, if not more, of a threat to the status quo than the rebel Perkin Warbeck and other Yorkist traitors had ever done. It was not because they had designs on the throne but was simply the result of their ability to give the new king exactly what he wanted – money, wealth, flattery and flamboyant status.

Foxe could not afford to let Empson and Dudley gain the King's ear, as they had done with his father. Once 'in' with the new monarch there would have been no end to their ability to control every aspect of English life. Hated as they were, continuation of their 'rule' would lead only to further discontent from the public and probably to an eventual rebellion. It would also have left Foxe and his friends high and dry.

As a consequence, at the moment of Henry VII's death, Bishop Foxe put into operation a plan which had been forming in his head for the previous few weeks, ever since it became clear King Henry's end was close.

Just two days away, on 24 April – St George's Day – the feast of the Order of the Garter was due to take place. A time when the 'great and the good' of the kingdom would gather to celebrate and give thanks for the reign of Henry, the Feast of the Garter was perhaps the most important courtly event of the year. It was also the only time in the immediate future when barons and earls of the country would come together in such numbers.

Until St George's Day, Foxe declared, news of the king's death would have to be kept secret. It would be known only to the men who had waited and watched around the bed of the dying king at the palace in Richmond. And that group certainly did not include Empson and Dudley.

Richard Foxe wanted and needed a united front. The reign of Henry VII had certainly brought the Wars of the Roses to an end but for all twenty-four years of his reign, the possibility of widespread unrest had still been hovering below the horizon.

Henry had ridden it all, fought when it was right to fight, negotiated when it was time to talk. He had done it well and he had enriched the country again after the depredations of the Wars of the Roses had reduced the economy virtually to zero. Through Empson and Dudley, he had made the crown financially secure and laid the foundations for a great dynasty.

The security provided by Henry, Empson and Dudley was not something that was ever really understood or appreciated by the majority of the English people. Traditionally 'one-eyed,' the populace viewed Henry's careful management of the fiscal situation as simply one more example of his avarice and miserly personality. From the highest in the land to the lowliest peasant at his farm gate, grumbling and regret were the order of the day.

The public view of the king was one of annoyance, even perhaps disappointment. For Empson and Dudley, there was only hatred. The public of both England and Wales was not strong enough, was too divided and distant, to do anything about them and for the moment, at least, people had to content themselves with grumbling.

Grumbling was almost an occupation in itself, something everybody did. But Bishop Richard Foxe knew that grumbling about conditions, about rules and laws, taxes and other impositions, was only one step away from actually doing something about them. All it needed was one strong man to pull the grumblers together and the result would have been open rebellion.

Now, with the death of the king, the dynasty had the possibility of entering a dynamic new period. Foxe was intent on ensuring it stayed that way. The new king was a popular and charismatic figure, tall and handsome with a love of splendour and pageantry. The very antithesis of his careful, abstemious father, he was an ideal front man.

But as yet Henry VIII was untried, untested. It would not take much for the fickle English public to turn against him. The alternatives, in the shape of Yorkist claimants, were there, lying low and awaiting their moment.

As far as Foxe was concerned, a united front of the nobles and men of significance was essential. Only by working together rather than in the traditionally isolated, ad hoc way usually presented by the nobility, could they avoid catastrophe and round up those whose loyalty to the regime remained unclear or undecided.

Equally as worrying, the new king's love of hunting and jousting, of clothes and palaces, of art and fine living made him a perfect target for Empson and Dudley. Unless somebody intervened, they could – and probably would – offer to act on his behalf and provide Henry with exactly what he desired most from his new role.

It was a delicate and dangerous time but Foxe had played the game of politics too long to miss his chance. If it all worked out as he hoped it would, his scheme would kill two birds with one stone.

Foxe was not afraid of Empson and Dudley – their power and potential for trouble, yes, that he could see and appreciate but he had little use or concern about them as individuals. If left unchecked, he viewed them as a possible threat to his position but more importantly, he saw them merely as pawns to be played with and then sacrificed. As Thomas Penn has written, they were the perfect scapegoats – 'Empson and Dudley had to go'.[7]

As far as Bishop Foxe was concerned the best way to achieve the ideal handover from one king to another was to give the English people exactly what they wanted – in this case, the heads of Empson and Dudley. It would be an offering to the people, a gift from their beloved new king.

The gift would come with an assurance. The ways of the old regime – spies and informers, taxes and draconian methods of control – would die with Henry VII. A new monarch would provide a new approach both to governance and to keeping his people happy.

* * *

While Foxe and his comrades plotted, Empson and Dudley took only minimal precautions to deal with the likely effects of the death of their benefactor. Whatever fears they may have held regarding the inevitable demise of the king they still felt safe and in control. Nothing would change, they believed, their services were indispensable.

In fact, the two lawyers had gravely misjudged the situation. While they believed that they had retained the friendship of people like Foxe and Lovell, even Lady Margaret Beaufort, mother of the dying king, nothing could be further from the truth.

Despite old age, Lady Margaret Beaufort was still a highly influential figure who had trodden many delicate paths in her efforts to bring her son to the throne and now, for the first few weeks of her grandson's reign, she would have to act as regent as he was still not yet in his majority. That, more than anything, made her a deadly enemy for the two extortionists.

In hindsight, it is amazing to think that Empson and Dudley should have been so naïve and trusting. The influence and help of their 'friends' would surely be enough to carry them through the transition, the pair seemed to think. Wouldn't they? The obvious answer to what was almost a rhetorical question was simple. No, they would not!

Almost to the end of what was a significant political crisis these two highly intelligent and capable counsellors were stunningly oblivious to the precariousness of their position. They had achieved their success with ease and their positions of power meant that they considered themselves above the machinations of people like Richard Foxe.

They had built up a highly effective spy ring which, normally, kept them well informed about the state of the nation but, for the moment at least, there was no news about what they really wanted to hear. Foxe had effectively closed down all communications to and from the palace at Richmond and news of the king's death remained a closely guarded secret. All Empson and Dudley received were dubious pieces of scanty and largely irrelevant information.

There were rumours, of course – the king was dying, the king was already dead, there was about to be a palace coup. In the light of these, both Empson and Dudley finally began to have concerns about the situation and, at the last moment, started to gather together retainers who would be capable of fighting on their behalf if uprisings should occur. It was too little and too late.

Both Empson and Dudley thought that any rebellions which did erupt would be the brainchild of some Yorkist claimant. Neither of them had bargained on trouble coming from within. The result was that they kept their faith in Foxe until the very end.

And when the time was right, Foxe struck with frightening rapidity. In the early hours of St George's Day, with the support of Britain's elite behind him, Foxe gave orders that several prominent members of the 'other camp' should be arrested. In its own way what happened that day was as cruel and crooked as anything Empson and Dudley had ever done. Yet Foxe, with Henry running behind him, had deemed it a necessary evil.

The arrested men included Henry Stafford, brother of the Duke of Buckingham, who was taken into custody simply because he might prove dangerous at some stage in the future. And of course, there were the prime targets, Richard Empson and Edmund Dudley.

At first light on 24 April heavily armed royalist troops were shuttled from Richmond to London, travelling silently and swiftly down the Thames on barges. Before the occupants of Empson and Dudley's houses were fully awake, they surrounded the two properties. Surprise was complete. The two men, shocked and frightened out of their wits, were arrested and taken to the Tower of London.

With Empson and Dudley safely imprisoned, news of Henry VII's death was announced later the same morning. Most people had been expecting it and so the news did not come as too great a shock. Quite the contrary, people welcomed the arrival of a new monarch.

The following day the new king made a triumphal progress through London to lodge, as tradition expected, in the Tower – a rather different part of the Tower from where Empson and Dudley were now residing. The streets were patrolled by columns of royalist soldiers who kept a surreptitious distance away from the front of the crowd but Henry's journey was greeted by cheering multitudes, confirming his popularity with the people. Foxe, Wolsey and the others noted the acclaim, nodded knowingly to themselves and stored it away for future use.

When, a few days later, the traditional Royal Pardon was issued, there was even more celebration. The Pardon, outlining the intentions of the new king, stressed that justice, so obviously lacking over the previous few years, would now be restored. More importantly, by including such a promise in the Pardon the crown was guaranteeing to honour and abide by the statement.

Henry's popularity soared yet again when on 11 June 1509 he married the Dowager Princess of Wales, Catherine of Aragon. Exquisitely beautiful, pious and blessed with 'the common touch', Catherine's previous marriage to Henry's brother Arthur had been declared invalid by Pope Julius and to the people of England and Wales, the union of the two most beautiful people in the kingdom seemed both natural and right.

It was an amazing start to Henry's reign, a start which had been created by his personality, by his marriage and, even more so, by the deliberate sacrifice of two of the previous monarch's most trusted companions and servants. It was nothing more than Bishop Foxe and Henry himself had desired and expected.

As part of the Royal Pardon, dozens of prisoners who had been held on the orders of Empson and Dudley were released from captivity – more celebrations and acclaim for the new king! Spies and informants like the merchant John Camby and the financier Henry Toft, both of whom had willingly sat on the rigged juries of the disgraced duo, now found themselves replacing their victims in the cells of London's prisons.

Some, like John Baptiste Grimaldi – a man almost as hated as Empson and Dudley – had read the situation rather better than his employers and decided that discretion was the better part of valour. A banker by trade but informer and spy at heart, Grimaldi fled to Westminster Abbey where he claimed sanctuary within the church. Safe inside the abbey he may have been uncomfortable but he was also untouchable, even by the new king.

Grimaldi, like so many others, was later pardoned by Henry but that was not the point. The arrest or persecution of men such as Grimaldi, Camby and Toft within days of his succession had hit the right note with the people who applauded and became almost delirious at the actions of their new king. Henry was clever and astute enough to note the emotions of the populace and, perhaps more importantly, to see how quickly those emotions could change. The London mob, he decided, was a fickle and highly dangerous unit.

For Empson and Dudley, there was to be no such reprieve. Their fate had already been decided. In July 1509, just two months after their fall, they were put on trial and to the surprise of no one were found guilty of what was euphemistically called 'constructive treason'.

The two men had planned to hold and guide the king and his council – or so the charge read, although there was scanty evidence to back up the claim – thus effectively seizing control of the country. A rigged jury handed down the only possible penalty. Death by beheading. Moral indignation would have allowed no other verdict.

That was not quite the end of things. The atmosphere at the king's court and palace was very different from the party atmosphere of the city. Fear was rampant as men looked anxiously over their shoulders, knowing that anyone who had ever had dealings with Empson and Dudley might well be next on the list of victims.

For most of them, the danger quickly passed. For some, men like William Smith, groom of Henry VII's wardrobe, along with Sir John Hussey, counsellor and friend of Edmund Dudley, the Tower soon beckoned. Dozens more quickly joined them as Henry's 'Night of the Long Knives' worked itself out.[8]

Empson and Dudley accepted their fate. They had little option. Their supporters, paid supporters after all, had seen the writing on the wall and had either fled or been flung into prison.

Any normal individuals would have looked for help or support from the general public. Empson and Dudley were far from normal prisoners. The only person they could have appealed to, the old king, was dead and buried. As for the public, there were precious few of them who would not have happily seen the duo torn limb from limb. All that was left to them was the executioner's axe.

Edmund Dudley spent the time between sentencing and execution writing a book, *The Tree of Commonwealth*. The book was to be his epitaph, his view of a life that he considered largely productive and useful.

It was also a diatribe about the way the country should be ruled and included a clear side-swipe at the manner in which things had been done in the previous reign. It probably gave Dudley a degree of satisfaction to subtly and without direct accusation, criticise the man who had given him so much power and then allowed him to suffer accordingly.

Sitting in the Tower, Dudley knew he had only a few months to live and there was no point in wallowing in self-pity. Right or wrong, he had done what his master had wanted and with a light sense of irony that contrasted beautifully with the barbarity of his time in power, he was at least able to smile at his fate:

> Furst ye must have the roote of Justice, without which the tree of the common wealth cannot contynew.[9]

Justice was probably the last thing on Edmund Dudley's mind, either while he was money-grabbing for the king or waiting with dread for the reward which many thought he so richly deserved.

It is doubtful that Henry VIII ever read the book. If he did, he certainly made no comment about it. The irony would not have been lost on him.

Richard Empson and Edmund Dudley were executed on 18 August 1510. Their demise was witnessed by crowds of howling Londoners, all delighted to see the hated pair get their just deserts. Deserved or not, their execution put the first troublesome disturbance of Henry's reign firmly to bed. At this stage in his royal career, he could clearly do nothing wrong.

Chapter Two

War, Glorious War

With Empson and Dudley imprisoned in the Tower and awaiting execution, Bishop Foxe and his new royal master felt it was time to take stock and decide what else could be done to keep the embryonic regime popular with the British public. Retaining the favour of their subjects was all-important to the ego-driven Tudors who had seen individual kings and whole dynasties, both in their own country and abroad, regularly come and go. A successful and acclaimed monarchy was crucial for the security of the whole nation.

Henry's father had made the crown incredibly rich. This was, in part, due to his abstemious ways but mainly thanks to the implementation of the brutal and dictatorial mini-regime under the auspices of the now-defunct Empson and Dudley.

Following the death of Henry VII, Bishop Foxe had 'sold' the new monarchy to the people on the ticket of change and, in particular, on the restoration of old liberties – old liberties which, really, had never been there in the first place. From now on, was the message, everything will be different – and we do mean everything. All of this ensured that the young Henry had been swept into the Palace of Westminster on a whirlwind of popular acclaim.

Foxe now had to grapple with the next problem – how to maintain the king's popularity once the initial fervour had worn off. Such fervour was as much mob hysteria as anything else and was always going to be short-lived. Given the character of the young Henry – as fickle as the London mob – reclaiming or reinventing it was, potentially at least, a significant problem.

In the public eye, the arrival of the new king in 1509 had heralded a 'new monarchy', a new beginning and a new age. Yet, new as it might seem to the people, the monarchy remained an institution that was founded on old traditions and old techniques. More than anything it was a regime that placed the same old reliance on the nobility of the country.

Like most other European countries there was, as yet, no professional civil service to undertake the running of the government. There was only the king and in order to manage the country effectively, he would have to work closely with his nobility, the very men who had achieved positions of responsibility under his father.

Unfortunately, from the start of his reign, it was clear that this particular example of royal leadership did not have the same dedication as his father. Nor did he have his predecessor's willingness to sacrifice his life to the family business!

What Henry needed was someone to take up the mantle of government, to run and control the country in his name. The obvious choice was Bishop Richard Foxe but by 1509 Foxe was nearly sixty years old and no longer so inclined to take on the aggressive requirements of the young king. His greatest political success had been in ensuring the succession of Henry VIII. It was now, perhaps, time to move on.

In modern parlance, Foxe hung in there but by 1511, two years after the succession, his star was clearly burning out as the old man turned more and more to the ecclesiastical and educational duties that he had so long ignored. They would be enough to occupy him for the rest of his old age! His crowning achievement during his final years was the founding of Corpus Christie College at Oxford but in old age, his sight failed him and he died peacefully in October 1528. Compared to the 'sticky endings' of those who followed him in the service of their king, Richard Foxe had been lucky.

Henry was equally as lucky, at least to begin with. There was already a new boy on the block, someone who was more than ready and waiting to pick up the mantle so recently discarded by Bishop Foxe.

Thomas Wolsey was hugely ambitious, the son of an Ipswich butcher and cattle dealer, a man whose lack of breeding and poor start in life was never going to be a problem on his road to success. He was a highly intelligent individual who quickly realised that for someone like him, without family connections to help him make a mark in the world, there was only one way to go. In order to advance his career and provide him with a suitable lifestyle, he would enter the church.

An ecclesiastical career was hardly a demanding profession for a man of Wolsey's talents and from the beginning of his work as a priest, he rose rapidly through the ranks. He was doing so well that by 1511 he had moved out of the orbit of the ordinary cleric – doing well, that is, in the service of the king rather than his God.

From the beginning of his career, Wolsey's ambitious rise was being noticed by the sages and wise men at court, many of them declaring that it was only the long life of William Warham, the current incumbent, which had prevented him from already being elevated to the post of Archbishop of Canterbury! It mattered not to Thomas Wolsey; a life 'in the cloth' had only ever been a means to an end for him. He had far greater aims in mind.

During his time as a student at Oxford, Wolsey had been befriended by the Marquis of Dorset, whose children he had mentored and tutored for a while. It was a good contact for Wolsey and the Marquis, impressed by his work ethic, had duly recommended the young clergyman to Henry VII as someone who could be both useful and trusted.

On Dorset's advice Henry had taken him up and before his death in 1509 had sent Wolsey on several diplomatic missions to the courts of Europe. He performed well in these various enterprises where his skill at diplomacy and an ability to talk with all manner of court officials and monarchs were reported back to Henry Tudor.

Not long before he died Henry made Wolsey an almoner and the following year the ambitious clergyman was elected a Knight of the Garter. Wolsey continued to be useful to Henry VII's successor so that just two years into the new king's reign he had already risen several rungs along the ladder of success.

His first major achievement, however, came in 1513 when, knowing Henry VIII's almost pathological desire for martial glory, Wolsey organised a subsidy to fund a huge army with which the king could invade the south-east of France.

The subsequent Battle of the Spurs, won by an exultant and happy Henry, saw the French flee in disarray and Tournai fall into English hands. Wolsey was rewarded by being made Bishop of Tournai, a position he held for only a short time before being elevated to the See of Lincoln. He was now firmly on his way!

After the defeat of the French Henry realised that he had found the man to front for him, to carry out the duties that were needed but which were hardly conducive to his lust for life. Delegation, Henry realised, was the answer to all his problems. And Wolsey wallowed happily in the mire of riches and splendour that were an inevitable accompaniment to working for Henry VIII.

The comparison with Empson and Dudley is hard to avoid but if Wolsey ever saw the similarity he never mentioned or spoke about it. The writer Polydore Vergil was another matter:

> When Wolsey attained the summit of his power, then he opened a law shop; what a Charybdis, what a whirlpool, what an abyss of every kind of plundering.[1]

By the time Vergil wrote the above passage, Wolsey was long dead but there were many who, reading the lines, albeit in hindsight, were more than able to appreciate the irony in the words.

Wolsey's rise was nothing short of stupendous. And having made his mark by raising the money for Henry's 1513 war with France he was set to continue. At that time and for the next twenty years, it was upwards all the way as far as Thomas Wolsey was concerned.

If he had to be a clergyman, he felt, he would have to be the top one and his determination to rule the English church saw Henry, at Wolsey's urging, persuade the Pope to make him a *legatus a latere* for life. This gave him the right to intervene – interfere many would have said – in every diocese in the land, over-ruling the lay and ecclesiastical decisions of bishops and archbishops as he chose.

He was aware of the many ecclesiastical wrongs of the time and initially vowed to do something about them. It was short term thinking, however, and eventually, Wolsey came to represent almost all of the abuses of the sixteenth-century church.

From absenteeism and pluralism to the misuse of legatine courts, from the propensity of priests to procure illegitimate children for themselves to amassing huge personal collections of art, gold and silver, Wolsey sampled them all. Whatever the faults or failings of the church Wolsey's involvement increased along with his girth!

In the eyes of the king, however, Wolsey could do no wrong. In 1515 Henry VIII, realising his immense political value, made him Lord Chancellor and that same year the Pope finally granted him a longed-for cardinal's hat. This meant that Thomas Wolsey, the butcher's boy from Ipswich, was now effectively head both of the church and the state in England and Wales. Arguably, he was already at the summit of his power.

*   *   *

For the first five or six years of his reign, Henry VIII relied heavily on the wave of affection and admiration that had accompanied his accession to the throne. Such love would, he felt sure, be enough to keep the people happy and content, basking in his magnificence.

Reality, however, was waiting in the wings and he soon began to realise that he could not live forever on the glory of the past. When food riots broke out in the distant west country it was something of a wake-up call for the king. Some of his people seemed to be unhappy.

Henry had been brought up on stories and legends of kings like the mythical Arthur, Richard the Lionheart and the Welsh warlords of the Mabinogion. The correlation was simple. Why should he not enjoy similar success in battle and let his people wallow in his glory?

Since his days as a prince of the realm, despite being tutored by men like the humanist scholar Erasmus, he had always harboured dreams of martial glory. In 1511, just two years after becoming king, Henry joined the Holy League of Spain, Venice and the Papacy in an alliance against France. As noted, in 1513 Wolsey funded the war and Henry sailed on blithely happy and content.

Everything appeared to be falling into place and the war which followed joining the Holy Alliance saw Henry's popularity increase even more. The people of Britain loved a good war, as long as they were not doing the actual fighting. War was good for profits and meant money in their pockets. It was also good for pride in their country and their king.

As it turned out, the conflict actually brought both success and failure to the English king. Despite his warlike dreams, Henry had only limited skill as a general. He was a great jouster and individual fighter but that meant very little in the wider world of generalship where a firm grasp of tactics and strategy were far more important than individual bravery.

A British victory at sea, the Battle of Brest, was offset by near-disaster at San Sebastian in June and July 1513 when King Ferdinand of Spain effectively abandoned Henry to his own devices, failing to provide the reinforcements and supplies he had promised. Not so much a battle as a 'standoff' that went on for some weeks, the San Sebastian debacle saw hundreds of English soldiers die, mainly from dysentery and other diseases.

The affair was kept largely hidden from the people at home and, in time, victories like the Battle of the Spurs which, in contrast to San Sebastian, was given maximum publicity, came to supersede it in importance. The Battle of the Spurs – named for the rapid escape of the French knights who showed their spurs rather than their chests to the English battle line – meant that back in England the king was now seen as a man of valour who was in the process of leading his armies to victory.

Against all rationale and defying any logical thought, the king's popularity grew even more when, on 5 August 1513, the Scots decided to take advantage of Henry's absence in Europe. On the orders of their king, James IV, a force of 7,000 reivers under the command of Lord Home crossed the border and began raiding English territories in the county of Northumberland.

In what became known as the *Ill Raid*, the Scots pillaged and plundered towns and villages across the length and breadth of Northumberland, burning houses and putting dozens of peasants to the sword. The invaders were soon laden down with plunder which, for most of the soldiers involved, was the sole purpose of the exercise.

Thomas Howard, Earl of Surrey, had already been appointed Lieutenant General of the Armies of the North and he reacted swiftly to news of the raid. The Scots might be interested mainly in pillage and plunder but Surrey had no desire to return to the days of Robert the Bruce when cross-border raiding had been a powerful weapon for the Scots.

He immediately sent a detachment of troops under the command of Sir William Bulmer to deal with the situation. Many of Bulmer's troops were mounted archers and when augmented by local levies the total strength of his army amounted to somewhere in the region of 1,000 men. It was powerful enough force but it was at least six or seven times smaller than Lord Home's border reivers.

Faced with such overwhelming numerical odds, Bulmer had to think carefully about how to deal with the situation. He was a wily warrior and decided that his best course of action was to catch the Scots in an ambush.

On 13 August, as the Scottish forces began to return home laden down with their spoils, he and his troops concealed themselves in the shoulder-high broom on Millfield Plain. And there they waited until the Scots came into view.

Their first volley of arrows took the raiders totally by surprise, killing as many as 600 before the English levies charged and slew many more.

The remaining reivers fled northwards, abandoning their booty which promptly found its way into the hands of Bulmer's troops rather than being returned to the rightful owners! *The Ill Raid* had cost the Scots dearly and the people of northern England rejoiced. But King James and his advisors were not discouraged by the English victory.

* * *

Franco-Scottish alliances had been commonplace since the days of Robert the Bruce when Scottish independence had been assured. Both Scotland and France had quickly become traditional enemies for England. Faced by the Holy League, King James IV of Scotland had allied his country with France as soon as Henry joined and that presented England with the possibility of a war on two fronts, a possibility that no one, least of all Henry, bothered about unduly – at least not until it happened.

The Ill Raid had been one thing, a full-scale invasion was a different matter altogether. It was not what was expected but acting on what he considered to be the laws and rules of chivalry, James IV sent Henry advance notice that he meant to invade northern England within the next month. Henry was campaigning with his armies in France but the warning still gave the English time to prepare themselves.

Henry's response to the Scottish announcement was immediate. On 11 August he received news of James' intentions, through a messenger, while he was engaged in the siege of Therouanne and promptly gave the Scottish herald a message to take back to his king:

If he be so hardy as to invade my realm or cause to enter one foot of my ground, I shall make him as weary of his parts as ever was a man that began such business.[2]

He then continued with the siege. Henry's wife, Catherine of Aragon, had been appointed regent in the king's absence and now she responded to the threat of invasion with an urgency that would have pleased Henry himself. The situation was far from easy, Catherine knowing that she had neither the time nor the inclination to call her husband back from France. She had to act and act quickly.

In Thomas Howard, Earl of Surrey, and his son, also called Thomas Howard, she had two very capable soldiers. In the coming days, she was going to need them.

Thomas Howard the Younger had already achieved success at sea by claiming a victory at the Battle of Brest but, like his father, he was always more comfortable fighting on land. He was about to receive plenty of opportunity as Catherine willingly gave the two Howard's a free hand in the north.

His message of intent having been delivered, James assembled an army that was, initially, over 40,000 strong. It was a mighty force of arms. Indeed, not since William of Normandy arrived in southern England in 1066 had there been such a significant incursion and everyone north of the border confidently predicted a Scottish victory.

The Scottish army was made up mainly of foot soldiers who were supported by small units of cavalry and a large number of cannons, gross culverins and other heavy artillery taken from Edinburgh Castle. The massive artillery pieces were dragged by teams of thirty or forty oxen and made slow progress across hillsides, rocks and rivers, the wheels of the gun limbers sometimes sinking up to their axles in the mud. Despite this, on 22 August the Scots crossed the River Tweed near Coldstream and, without opposition, sallied into England.

In the wake of the massive Scottish army fear spread like wildfire across northern England. The county of Northumberland, as a border province, was virtually a militarised zone and over the years its people had become used to being raided by the Scots This was different, however; this was a full-scale invasion and people automatically looked to their king to protect them from such a force. Many doubted his ability. This mighty host was surely unbeatable.

As so often before, looks were deceptive. To begin with, the Scottish army was not a paid force but, rather, was made up of men responding to a feudal obligation to serve their king for the relatively short period of just forty days. After that, they were free to go home.

There was also the matter of weaponry. The Scots were armed mainly with long pikes, weapons that had worked well for the French when fighting in open parkland against opponents like the Swiss but which were cumbersome and needed considerable practice in order to be effective in battle.

The English soldiers, by contrast, were armed mainly with bills or bill hooks, shorter and much more manoeuvrable in close-quarter actions. Deriving from agricultural implements of the same name, the bill hooks were lethal weapons that could be swung around the body, unlike the Scottish pikes which were mainly thrusting implements or weapons. Even an untrained, untried infantry soldier could bring down an opponent with just one strike of his bill hook.

Things began well for the Scots. James wasted no time before investing several of the English border castles where, using his heavy artillery, he battered the walls of Norham Castle. It fell after a six-day siege and the fortresses of Etal and Ford soon followed. In complete contrast to his earlier energy, James then spent several days entertaining and enjoying the company of Elizabeth, Lady Heron of Ford Castle. It was a delay that was soon to cost him dearly.

While James flirted with Lady Heron, Thomas Howard was camped at Pontefract. From there he issued orders for a general mustering at Newcastle. Unfortunately, his preparations were delayed by bad weather which kept his fleet at sea and lying off land for several days.

The fleet, under the command of Surrey's son, the Lord High Admiral of England, was an essential element in the English strategy. Apart from guarding the army's right flank, the ships were carrying the English artillery pieces, vital for countering the Scottish cannons. From an English point of view, the importance of their artillery made the delay understandable but if James had not been so intent on wasting his time at Ford and had attacked before Surrey was ready then the outcome of the battle which was soon to follow might have been very different.

The bad weather eventually abated and the fleet of Howard the Younger was at last able to make port. The cannons were unloaded and the English muster was eventually completed at Durham on 28 August.

Meanwhile, on 27 August Queen Catherine had issued warrants for the property of all Scotsmen living in England to be confiscated. Next, she ordered Thomas, Lord Lovell to raise an army in the Midlands to operate as a fail-safe should the Earl of Surrey meet with defeat. She then headed north, heavily pregnant and fully clad in armour, thereby foreshadowing by many years the appearance and attitude of Elizabeth during the famous Armada crisis.

Defeat was not on Surrey's mind. Having taken possession of his artillery pieces, he marched resolutely towards the army of King James which was now established at Flodden Edge, close to the border town of Berwick on Tweed.

Seeing the English approach James issued a challenge, inviting the English to engage in combat on the open ground in front of his army. The Earl of Surrey, knowing that he was greatly outnumbered, declined. James's force had decreased in size, due to sickness and desertion as men realised their forty-day enlistment was up and headed off for home. Even so, he still had more than 30,000 troops at his command – more than enough, he felt, to deal with the English.

Rather than risk a head-to-head confrontation, the Earl of Surrey took his soldiers on a circuitous route march that brought them along the Devil's Causeway to a position at the rear of the Scottish army. The battlefield had now swung around 360 degrees with the Scots occupying Branxton Hill, denying it to the English and facing their opponents across uncharted, unreconnoitered acres of land. It was a location where James had not expected to fight.

Even so, it was there, at 4.00 in the afternoon of 9 September 1513 that the action began. The coming battle was to be the largest and perhaps most brutal contest ever fought between Scotland and England.

The weather was wet and windy and the Battle of Flodden Field opened with an artillery duel between the two sides. For men like the Earl of Surrey who had fought at Bosworth in 1485, the similarity to the opening stages of the two battles was uncanny.

Unfortunately for the Scots, being based on top of a hill meant that their massive cannons were unable to lower their trajectory sufficiently to take out their opposing gunners. Their cannons could, at best, fire once every twenty minutes; the English artillery, although older and lighter, was able to open fire more quickly, changing position and targets at will. They therefore inflicted considerably more damage on the enemy ranks.

The opening gunfire was followed by hails of arrows from both sides before the Scots, never the most disciplined of warriors, charged downhill in an attempt to close with the enemy. It was no easy task, particularly as the long and unwieldy pikes somehow always seemed to be getting between the legs of the running men.

Things were made even more difficult when the Scots finally realised that the land between themselves and the English was not as flat and easily traversed as they had thought. It was, in fact, a marshy bog. The Scottish formations which relied on blocks of united soldiers, all moving forward together in rigid formation, were broken up by the marshy land.

The Earl of Surrey, seeing the chaos in the Scottish ranks seized his chance and sent in his infantry. With their bill hooks and swords, the English were always better equipped for close-quarter combat and it quickly became clear that they were gaining the upper hand.

King James, in a desperate attempt to shore up his lines, threw himself at the thickest part of the battle. He had been criticised many times for exposing himself to unnecessary danger in battle and this time the critics were proved right. Surrounded by his bodyguard – the Flowers of the Forest as they were known – he and most of his companions were cut down and killed.

James IV of Scotland was the last sovereign from the British Isles to die in combat. Inspection of his corpse later showed arrow wounds and huge slashes from bladed weapons on his front and on his back. It had been a heroic death.

In the wake of their king's death, the Scots were in despair and fled the field. The road back to Scotland was long and arduous and many were cut down or captured in their flight. Mostly, the English were happy to just watch them go.

Catherine of Aragon heard the news of the English victory while resting at Woburn Abbey where she had paused in her march northwards. She immediately sent a herald with a triumphant message announcing the success to her husband in France. Included in the package was a blood-stained piece of the coat worn by James at Flodden. Henry would, Catherine hoped, use it as a banner during his French campaign.

James IV had gambled and lost. Amazingly, the two incidents of Scottish invasion, far from destroying Henry's reputation, merely increased it, even though he wasn't even in the country at the time. The king will save us, Henry will throw back the Scots, that was the general consensus of opinion. He will come back, he must come back, our security depends on him!

True to his image and the expectations of his people, Henry *did* hurry home. However, it was more of an attempt to wallow in the glory of what was really Queen Catherine's victory, than a return in order to defeat James.

Even then Henry managed to get it wrong. Early in October, on his way back to England he contracted smallpox, a disease that was usually fatal but this time, in Henry's case, it was merely a debilitating illness. His constitution was strong, at least at this early stage of his life, and he recovered quickly.

All that remained for Henry to do now was to tie up loose ends. Realising that his Spanish allies had no intention of invading France, he made his own peace with the French king, ending a war that had brought him a suitable amount of glory, killed thousands of men and increased his reputation with his subjects.

Tournai was returned to the French, a gift that was no real sacrifice for the magnanimous Henry. Although further wars with the French were to erupt several times during his reign, Henry was happy that he had proved his manhood. He had fought his war and he had been victorious.

Part of the peace agreement was that Henry's young sister Mary should marry the aged Louis XII. The wedding took place in October 1513 and, much to the amusement of many French and British courtiers who were only too happy to slyly nudge each other and comment on old men and young brides, Louis died just two months later. He was worn out, the cynical sages declared, by the attentions of his young bride. Always conscious of the value attached to his sister, Henry promptly disregarded the normal period of mourning and married her off to the new Scottish king.

The death of Louis had been perhaps inevitable, given his age, but more importantly for Henry and the whole of Europe, it brought the young, flamboyant Francis I to the French throne.

As far as Henry and Francis were concerned it was mutual dislike at first glance. In hindsight, it is easy to see how and where that dislike originated. Both men were vain, pompous and unsure about their own identity as Renaissance princes. Both men were eager to secure centre stage. Henry now had a rival for the role as the most glamorous monarch in Europe and he did not like it, not one bit.

The relationship between the two kings deteriorated even further after the Field of Cloth of Gold, held on the edge of the Calais Pale – the only

English-held territory left in France – between 7 and 24 June 1520. This was effectively a summit meeting between the two kings and the two nations, the brainchild of Cardinal Wolsey.

Its main aim was to increase and tighten the bond of friendship between Henry and Francis but there were other intents and purposes, one of which was to outlaw war between the Christian nations of Europe. Even the rulers of the Ottoman Empire supported the enterprise although they clearly still harboured designs on the rich pasture land of Austria.

Despite these laudable aims the meeting rapidly deteriorated into an antagonistic display of magnificence by the English and the French delegations as men and women of both nations strove to outdo each other.

Apart from the formal competitions which were organised each day, there was great competition in debates and discussions about who had the best dress, the finest silks, the finest pack of hunting dogs and so on.

Despite all this, the Field of Cloth of Gold was a spectacular event, the like of which had never been seen before or was ever likely to be seen again. Nobody who was present, either as a guest or as an official, ever forgot the experience.

No expense was spared. Luxurious apartments lined with silk and gold cloth were erected for the two main rulers and over 2,000 tents were provided for the 'lesser' nobles and officials. It was a vast tented city of unbelievable splendour and grace.

The most notable attractions included two huge fountains which showered out red wine all day and night and a pair of tiny monkeys dressed in gold leaf and left to parade around the site. Inevitably they gravitated to wherever there were food and attention. The monkeys were the gift of Sultan Selim I of Turkey and were a particular favourite with King Francis.

Enormous and long-lasting feasts, jousting tournaments, dancing and music were all on the agenda as men and women paraded in their best and most flamboyant costumes. In theory, such a pantomime should have achieved its desired result but it was not to be.

Things turned particularly sour when, despite an injunction that the two monarchs would not compete with each other in any of the contests, Henry challenged Francis to a wrestling match – and lost!

The lighter, nimbler Frenchman apparently lured the bulky Henry into a bear-hug, then tripped him and threw him to the ground. Victory to the

French! To lose at anything was bad enough for Henry but to be defeated by this French upstart was something he found impossible to stomach. He never forgot the insult.

Henry went off in high dudgeon and Wolsey, obeying his master's orders, immediately signed a peace agreement with Charles V of Spain. Within a few months war was again declared on France. The vast expenditure of the Field of Cloth of Gold had been in vain.

There were two other wars against France during Henry's reign and a threat of invasion which in July 1545 saw the giant warship *Mary Rose* sink in the Solent. Such happenings were part and parcel of Henry's troubled and troublesome years as monarch. Yet almost to the last very few Englishmen ever knew that their king had once been beaten by Francis in a one-on-one wrestling match.

Chapter Three

Cleansing the Stables

With the Scottish threat nullified and a peace treaty signed with France, one factor became increasingly clear to Henry and his government officials. If he wanted to remain unchallenged at the top of the Tudor tree, then there were elements in English society that needed to be changed. At the very least they needed to be controlled, but preferably extinguished.

The top-heavy, autocratic regime of his father and of many previous monarchs before him, had served the country well but it was hardly suitable for the Renaissance prince that Henry purported to be. Some cleansing of the stables was clearly called for and there was a sufficiency of people who were willing to do it. *How* to do it, however, was another matter altogether.

There was, of course, the well-tried technique of arrest, imprisonment and, if necessary, execution. Bishop Richard Foxe had effectively used this on the day he announced the death of King Henry VII and had Empson and Dudley arrested.

Henry Stafford had also been incarcerated that morning for no other reason than, as the brother of the Duke of Buckingham, the most powerful noble in the land, he was a potential worry and concern. Unlike Empson and Dudley, Stafford was later released but, importantly, at the crisis point of Henry VIII's accession, the man was behind bars and out of the way. It was undoubtedly effective but it was a heavy-handed method of control, hardly geared to facilitate affection or any emotion apart from fear.

As with any autocratic regime which had its roots or origins buried in what was essentially the old feudal system, the possibility of internal conflict was always present during Henry's reign. Deadly emotions like resentment, greed and jealousy were always lurking in the bosoms of ambitious men who felt they could do better than the reigning monarch, whoever that might be. The potential for rebellion was an occupational hazard that was likely to keep recurring unless steps were taken to avoid it.

Henry and his 'management team' – effectively Henry and Wolsey – quickly came to regard conflict within the realm as a draining and ultimately self-destructive process. It was something which was to be avoided by the simple matter of the crown getting its retaliation in first. Despite the power of that phrase and contrary to his historical reputation, Henry was not always a 'blood and guts' tyrant who knew only one way to respond to a problem or challenge, at least not to begin with. He could and would listen to advice before making his decisions.

With his desire for military victory achieved, Henry's dreams of glory were, for the moment at least, sated. Now the king was more than happy to listen to Foxe, Wolsey and other notable statesmen like the humanist scholar Thomas More. He would turn his attention to the state of his nation. At first glance, everything seemed fine but it did not do to ignore the people for too long. They were nothing if not fickle, well able to change their allegiance and behaviour in the blink of an eye.

Foxe, Henry and, in due course, Thomas Wolsey were all astute enough to realise it was not always in the best interests of the regime to go around arresting and executing men at will. Such an approach would undoubtedly take out the more dangerous elements in the country but it also involved the very real risk of alienating large sections of the nobility and gentry. And that could eventually lead to rebellion on a grand scale.

So, how to proceed? Henry and his advisors came to the conclusion that beating only ever produced bruises and resentment and the men they needed to govern the state would respond far better to the bribe or the carrot than they ever would to the stick. The up and down career of Thomas Howard, the Earl of Surrey was a classic case in point.

Howard had forfeited his titles, his lands and his freedom after fighting for Richard III against Henry's father at the Battle of Bosworth Field. In the wake of Richard's defeat, Howard was immediately incarcerated in the Tower and was lucky not to lose his head.

Later reprieved and released from the Tower after refusing to join a rebellion against Henry VII, Howard was still not given back all his lands or his main title as Duke of Norfolk until he had proved his loyalty to the Tudor dynasty. This he did by defeating the Scots at Flodden but until then he would remain Earl of Surrey. After his victory, baronetcy restored, Thomas Howard continued to serve the king until disaster struck again.

The uncle of two of Henry's wives, Anne Boleyn and Catherine Howard, and with his main title of Duke of Norfolk restored to him, Thomas Howard was given a significant role at court. He came to occupy the position of Henry's strong right arm, the man who could be despatched to solve almost any military or rebellious problem.

However, after the execution of the flighty Catherine Howard, he fell out of favour. In 1546 he was stripped of his dukedom and sent to the Tower. He was saved from execution only by the death of Henry in January 1547. It had been a career of highs and lows, one which typified the life and times of the nobility in the reign of Henry VIII.

Tudor society was hierarchical in nature. The king stood at the top, ruling by Divine Right, while the peasants sat firmly at the bottom with precious few rights at all. In between were the nobles, the gentry, knights and yeomen.

Although chosen by God and therefore able to rule as he chose, the king still needed the support of the nobility in order to run the country. Memories of the Wars of the Roses when the monarch could clearly not control the barons and earls of England were too close for comfort. A strategy was needed, one which, while maintaining the structure of the kingdom, would keep disruption and disorder to the bare minimum.

Consequently, what developed was an ingenious and highly effective way of ridding the country of disaffected elements, a way of cleansing the stables that was both inclusive and compelling. It was a two-pronged approach to the avoidance of disorder – the deliberate use of patronage and the introduction of royal progresses.

Both techniques were positive, as opposed to the negative approach of arrest, torture and the inevitable demise of the captive. Control was to be achieved not by cutting out the cancer but by keeping it in its place!

There would still be treason trials while executions would remain commonplace events, even if only for those who, in the mind of the king, deserved it. However, the increasing use of patronage and progresses as methods of control were invariably more humane processes and often just as successful. They were policies of inclusion rather than exclusion. So, what were they and how exactly did they work?

Henry VII had disliked and distrusted his nobles but he knew, from the start of his reign, that he needed them. His distrust was understandable, he was little more than a disgruntled earl himself and the prospect of somebody doing what he had done, rebelling and usurping the throne, was always there, no matter how distant a prospect it eventually became. In his regime, it was up to the nobles to work, and work hard, in order to gain the trust of the king. Then – and only then – were they rewarded with positions of trust.

Henry VIII was different. He had no particular love for the aristocracy and his relationship with his advisors came to depend more and more on patronage which both he and the recipients saw as his divine gift. Simply having a grand title was never going to be enough to secure a high position. What gradually emerged was an early form of meritocracy – prove that you could do the job and it was yours!

Henry would reward his friends and colleagues, many of them men with whom he hunted and competed against in the lists, for their service and their advice. A large number of them were from fairly low and humble backgrounds, further proof that it was ability rather than breeding or ownership of grand titles and estates which ensured the king's favour.

It was an approach that began a slow and steady change in the balance of power so that by the end of Henry's reign, the nobility was still important but there were now far greater opportunities for men of poorer origins:

> Power and influence were dictated by the ability to gain access to Henry or to one of his chief ministers ... This led to the development of a group of men who owed their positions to their influence at Court rather than because of their landed estates.[1]

The obvious examples were Cromwell and Wolsey but there were many more, at all stages and levels of royal governance. These were men who realised that through patronage from the king they could make their way in society and at court, despite their humble beginnings and backgrounds. They came to hold posts like Groom of the Stool and Gentlemen of the Chamber, intimate and privileged positions where their relationships with the king were private, long-lasting and intense. Their loyalty was assured.

Inevitably, there were downsides to the concept of patronage. Unless it was carefully watched it could easily lead to the growth of factions and to jealousy amongst the king's closest supporters. When it came to the really big issues of the day, matters such as Henry's religious settlement, there was a genuine potential for serious division. As Wolsey and Cromwell soon realised, it needed careful monitoring. Even then, both men got it wrong, as we shall see!

The art of running royal progresses was a simple case of maintaining the popularity of the king by keeping him in the view of his people. Let everyone from the highest noble in the land to the lowest beggar and serf in his miserable cottage see that this was a monarch who had their interests at heart but who, more importantly, was available to be seen and touched. It was a myth, of course, a total and complete lie. Anyone who got within ten yards of the monarch would have been instantly cut down. But it was a good myth and the people fell for it.

An effective progress was proof of the King's popularity, the simple if hugely expensive process of the king and his court progressing around the land and showing themselves to the people – in other words displaying the common touch to maintain the monarch's popularity. Neither Henry nor his advisors could ever forget the fervour surrounding his accession to the throne, the screaming crowds and waves of love that flowed from the populace. A progress was one way of repeating that outpouring of affection.

In the days before newspapers and photography very few of his subjects, apart from the nobles, actually knew what King Henry looked like. They might have glanced at his image on some of the coins of the realm but that would have been all. So, to see him suddenly in their village or town, in their midst, was both a thrill and an education for the king's subjects.

A royal progress was a method of displaying the power and the wealth of the court. It smacked of military might but it put the people in close personal touch with the monarch. The progresses were huge affairs, sometimes involving as many as 1,000 servants, advisors, nobles and officials and lasting for weeks on end.

In the main, progresses were aimed at distant parts of the realm, areas which were often forgotten or ignored in the daily running of the country. Londoners were used to seeing the king as he went about his daily life, the residents of Cornwall or Yorkshire were not.

To those who lived in what was, in Tudor times, almost rural isolation Henry was almost a mythical figure, a man of celebratory status and stature. A progress was a way of showing the people that their king was as grand as they had always imagined. It was, therefore, important that he came up to the mark when he showed himself to his subjects.

The progresses were magnificent displays of pomp, about as far removed from Henry VII's method of ruling as the dark side of the moon. But then, Henry VIII was a very different sort of man from his father.

Not only did a royal progress increase the popularity of the king, it enabled the nobles to see what the king's subjects felt about their ruler. Remember this adulation, these waves of affection, that was the implicit message. It is not something that *you* could ever achieve or replicate. It was a warning that was never spoken or declared but the hint was there.

A royal progress was also a time when people could present grievances and complaints in the hope of gaining justice, a time when they could – metaphorically at least – reach out and get in touch with their monarch:

> This summer the King took his progress westwards and visited his towns and castles there, and heard the complaints of his poor commonality and ever as he rode, he hunted and liberally departed with venison.[2]

Patronage and progress were important elements in the life and role of the royal court and the governing of the country. Yet they could not exist in isolation and many of the other techniques employed by the government were considerably more intrusive, even punitive. The use of subsidies was just one of them.

Cardinal Wolsey was the prime mover behind the concept of subsidies. They began in 1513 when he was forced to find new ways of raising money for Henry's war with France. The Commons was not in the best of moods to grant the king money to spend on fripperies like war:

> They had subsidised the wars of Henry VII without complaining because the demands made on them were infrequent and relatively light and because they approved of his policies. Henry VIII's campaigns, however, were inspired by no obvious need. They were widely recognised as Wolsey's wars and there was great resentment at the sums of money demanded.[3]

Henry was adamant. He *would* go to war and as a consequence over £1 million was spent on campaigning in the first ten years of his reign. That was a huge sum of money when the monarchy only received £25,000 a year from its normal tax sources. Finding a way to make up the deficit was Wolsey's problem and he did not flinch at the task.

A subsidy was a flexible tax where each individual was assessed on their income from land or profession and from the value of their possessions.

This was markedly different from previous assessments where taxes were fixed, Boroughs paying one-tenth of their saleable goods or products, countryside locations one-fifteenth of the value of their goods grown and produced each year.

The old process might have avoided the problem of working out annual tax assessments but the system was long out of date. Communities were paying levels of tax that had been set a hundred or even two hundred years before and which made no allowance for good or bad harvests, the vagaries of war and so on.

Not surprisingly, the subsidy system met with the approval of Parliament. This was simply because it affected the Members of Parliament more than anyone else, reducing the amount of resentment caused by the old tenth and fifteenth arrangements. That resentment came mainly from the middling and moneyed classes, the very men who sat in the Commons.

Agreement from one significant group was matched by anger from another. Above all, Wolsey's idea of subsidies ensured that the wealthier elements in society paid more in tax than their poorer colleagues, something that seemed fair to the men in the Commons, but not to the great nobles of the land. By levying the tax only when it was needed, as opposed to a regular imposition, by 1523 Wolsey had raised over £300,000. The old tax system, which still continued, brought in less than a third of that total.[4]

The subsidy system was a clever way of keeping disgruntlement in check and worked well with the system of patronage and progression. Until, that is, the subsidies became too regular and too demanding. It did, also, create a broad band of disapproval and discontent from men who grew to hate Wolsey more and more every year. The nobles of England would wait for their moment but when it finally came it was both brutal and lasting.

* * *

And what of those who resisted the efforts of Cromwell and Wolsey to keep them within the confines of Tudor law and order? There was, really, only one recourse and the executioners of England were kept busy throughout the thirty-nine years Henry sat on the throne.

Despite his reputation as 'the killer king' there were actually far fewer executions during Henry's reign than was originally believed. At the same time, he was no 'milksop monarch'. He would do what he had to do and those who went 'Beyond the Pale' of justice and obedience to their king were severely dealt with.

Estimates vary regarding the number of people he had killed. For a long while, a figure of 80,000 was bandied about. It was a gross exaggeration. Such a figure would have meant exterminating somewhere in the region of one-fifth of the whole population of the country. Modern estimates now put the number of executions during Henry's reign at approximately 800.

Those who did succumb to the final punishment included noblemen, knights, peasants, members of the clergy and some of the king's closest allies. Such was the power and the paranoia of the king that it sometimes seemed as if a fall from grace and an eventual meeting with the executioner's axe were inevitabilities for anyone who aspired to high office in Henry's England. Clearly, however, men – and, as it turned out, women as well – felt the risk was balanced out by the rewards.

And it was a very real risk. Cardinal Wolsey was lucky to escape the block, dying on his way to imprisonment in the Tower. Two of the king's wives were beheaded while Sir Thomas More and Thomas Cromwell were both executed as a result of the strange mind-workings of the most ungenerous and unforgiving monarch ever to rule the kingdom. Henry was known to regret the deaths of both More and Cromwell but execution was a one-way affair. Once put into operation there was no way back.

There were reasons for all of the executions during his reign, at least in the mind of Henry. He killed or had killed members of his family, close advisors and dozens of people he never actually met but who had offended against the state. These were, perhaps, not particularly valid or reasonable reasons for the punishments, at least by modern standards, but the executions do have to be considered in the context of the times.

The overriding cause or reason behind the executions was always to maintain order and eliminate the possibility of disturbance in the kingdom. Keeping the peace, maintaining the status quo, was the single driving factor behind so many of the policies and actions during Henry's reign.

It was a brutal age but it was also a time when the peace of the nation hung by a thread. Henry, like all medieval rulers, knew that he had to act with care and diligence – but at the same time with a vitality that bordered on savagery.

There was no middle course for those who had offended the state – forgive or execute, those were the options. Even men and women who found themselves incarcerated in gaol knew that while such imprisonment might seem as if it was running on forever, sooner or later their turn would come and the executioner's axe would fall.

A variety of different methods were used for executions. Normally, it was a case of hanging for commoners, beheading for people of noble birth. They were effective enough but neither of them was a particularly clean death.

Hanging invariably involved slow strangulation; only rarely was the unfortunate victim's neck broken in the fall. It sometimes took up to half an hour for a hanged man or woman to die, the agony of those final minutes being seen as part of the punishment.

Depending on the skill of the axeman, beheading usually took three or four blows of the axe to sever the head from the body. Occasionally a botched execution saw as many as six, seven or even eight attempts to finish off the condemned person, hardly surprising given the inappropriateness of the axe and the block. Deaths like that of Queen Anne Boleyn where a French swordsman was brought in to ensure a swift, single-stroke ending were exceptionally rare.

So much for the more refined methods of punishment. Greater crimes meant more brutal methods of execution. For those found guilty of treason, the punishment was truly horrific. It involved the ghastly process of hanging, drawing and quartering. And that was a million times worse than either hanging or beheading.

Such executions involved the victim being strung up but lowered to the ground, half-conscious, before expiring. Disembowelling whilst still alive, castration and displaying of the still-beating heart to the crowd were followed by merciful decapitation and death. It is hard to know how long the victims remained conscious and aware of what was happening to them as shock and trauma must have hit at some stage of the process.

Other methods of execution were equally as gruesome. These included pressing, being boiled alive and burning at the stake. Pressing involved a plank of wood being laid across the prostrate body of the victim. Heavy stones or weights were then placed onto the body which restricted breathing and eventually resulted in suffocation.

The horrific punishment of boiling alive was reserved specifically for poisoners and was only used once in Henry's reign. It was exactly what the term suggested, the victim being placed in a large metal container, a fire being lit beneath it and the condemned man being slowly boiled alive.

Burning at the stake, the traditional fate for heretics, was employed all over Europe by the Catholic Church, the concept of burning the 'guilty' person being linked with the whole idea of perishing in the fires of Hell. The number of official burnings at the stake reached its apogee in the reign of Henry's daughter Mary but there were enough gruesome burnings in the king's reign to keep executioners and the baying members of the public more than happy.

Such burning might end quickly if the friends and family of the accused could persuade – and pay – the chief executioner to conceal a small bag of gunpowder somewhere under the clothing of the condemned person. Once the flames reached the gunpowder it would explode, killing the victim considerably quicker than the smoke and heat of the fire. Quite what the hundreds of spectators thought about such a merciful end has not been recorded.

Most executions were public affairs, announced in advance and with thousands flocking to watch the final moments of the unlucky victim. They were days of great enjoyment for the public, a carnival atmosphere pervading each execution site.

Pie sellers and pamphleteers plied their wares, jugglers and acrobats vied for attention and people often began queuing before dawn in order to get the best view. Nobles and royal victims like Anne Boleyn and Catherine Howard were awarded the 'privilege' of a private demise. For most people, however, there was no such favour.

Executions were considered to be educational, for the spectators at least, and there is no doubt that witnessing someone being hanged, drawn and quartered was something that would stay with you for the rest of your life. The blood and the brutality did not stop executions being popular affairs. A day out at the executions? Life, like death, was cheap in Tudor England.

Chapter Four

For Those About to Die –
the Rise or Fall of Paranoia

Henry's descent into paranoia is now an accepted fact. The longer his reign went on the more obvious those paranoid tensions became. However, signs of such emotions were there from the earliest days of his rule and were part and parcel of a troublesome period in history and of a charismatic but thoroughly dangerous monarch.

Throughout his life and, in particular, for the full extent of his reign the fear of a Yorkist rising or revolt never quite left Henry's mind. He knew that the Tudor dynasty had come to power by the strength of the sword rather than through any specific and particular right to the Crown. In what was a clear case of might over right, his father had been a usurper and that stigma undoubtedly played on the mind of the young Henry.

Henry was haunted by the knowledge that there were several alternative claimants to the throne, men who had a somewhat better right to be king than him. In his mind, the remnants of the House of York offered the greatest threat to his embryonic rule which meant of course that, like Empson and Dudley before them, the time of such men on earth– King Henry's earth, at least – was limited. That applied even if they had no intention of ever challenging Henry's right to rule.

In the person of Edmund de la Pole, the Earl of Suffolk, Henry had a perfect target. And to assist him in taking hold of the man in question, Henry did not actually need to go hunting for his quarry. Edmund de la Pole was already in his power and easily accessible. He was in the Tower of London.

Edmund was the son of Elizabeth of York, a sister of King Richard III, and of John de la Pole, the second Earl of Suffolk. John had hitched his star to the pretender Lambert Simnel during the reign of Henry VII and had paid the ultimate price for the failure of that particular plot.

After the execution of the Earl of Warwick, who met his end on the scaffold with Perkin Warbeck in 1499, Edmund became the leading Yorkist claimant to the throne. However, with the Tudors now established in power, it was an empty accolade, a matter of prestige that really bothered no one apart from the paranoid Henry VIII. To him, however, it was enough to make Pole a real and dangerous threat to the Tudor dynasty.

Edmund de la Pole had led a varied and adventurous life. He had defended the Tudor regime against Cornish rebels in 1497 but then had a change of heart and subsequently, without permission of the Crown, left the kingdom in 1501.

Once established on the continent Edmund de la Pole joined forces with Maximilian, then the Holy Roman Emperor, adopting the title 'The White Rose' in order to display his Yorkist background and membership of the Yorkist line. It was another meaningless gesture but as a consequence, in 1502, Henry VII had him declared an outlaw.

After four years of being embroiled in the politics of Europe, in 1506 Edmund became a prisoner of Phillip, Archduke of Burgundy. It was a civilised captivity, not dissimilar to Henry Tudor's own period in exile, but that same year Phillip's ship, en route to Spain to claim his wife's dowry, was blown off course and ended up on the coast of England. Phillip was now a 'guest' of Henry VII – who immediately offered him freedom as long as he would hand over Edmund de la Pole.

The deal was swiftly done. Within a short space of time, Edmund found himself back in England, confined in the Tower of London. And that was where he lay for the next half dozen years. As far as the first of the Tudor monarchs was concerned, Edmund de la Pole was seemingly safe enough, out of harm's way and held where he could cause little trouble. Edmund, on the other hand, probably had nightly dreams of what glories might still come to fruition – mingled, of course, with the inevitable fear of death and destruction.

When Henry VIII became king in 1509 Edmund de la Pole was still in the Tower. He and many others confidently expected to be released as part of the traditional Royal Pardon given to prisoners by all new kings. After all, he had spent seven years in incarceration and had shown no inclination to escape or undermine the Tudor dynasty. Freedom surely beckoned.

Unfortunately for Edmund, his brother Richard de la Pole had recently joined the service of France, England's traditional enemy. That, in Henry's paranoid brain, showed him exactly where the Pole loyalties really lay. As a result, when the King's Pardon was announced Edmund found himself exempted. His captivity would continue. It was a bitter blow but there was worse to come. It began with a further four years kicking his heels in the Tower.

Henry did not agree with his father's concept of playing the 'long game'. He could not forget the significance of his prisoner, however hard he tried and the thought of a potential Yorkist opponent lying within his grasp was more than he could bear.

As the leading Yorkist claimant to the throne Pole was, potentially, too big a threat for Henry to even consider granting him his freedom. It was only a matter of time but what soon happened would show the king's latent ruthlessness and mark one of the earliest signs of paranoia in his personality.

Knowing he had Pole at his mercy Henry took what he considered the only possible course of action. Without ever having engaged in any form of treason against the Crown and without even being given the benefit of a trial, on 13 April 1513 Edmund de la Pole was taken from the Tower and immediately beheaded. He was not even graced by the dignity of a charge – if ever there was a case of judicial murder, then this was it.

Edmund de la Pole was hardly part of the disorder and disturbance to the land that Henry so feared but, rather, it was his potential for trouble that was the problem. Even in captivity, as long as the man was alive there was always the possibility that disorderly elements would rise up in his name and overturn the Tudor monarchy.

The Pole family continued to be an itch that Henry could not scratch. They were some of the last remnants of the Yorkist threat – or, rather, the perceived Yorkist threat – and later in his reign, the king would return to the problem and wipe them out. For the moment, though, his desire to deal with this troubled and troublesome element of his nation had been fulfilled.

* * *

Edmund de la Pole was not the only early victim of Henry's gradual but steadily growing paranoia. Edward Stafford, the third Duke of Buckingham, was the most powerful nobleman in England after the king and although it was never a step he never actually took, he was one of the few men in the kingdom who could have legitimately challenged Henry's right to the throne. He could certainly have been an alternative monarch if Henry had died without children.

Stafford/Buckingham was actually a cousin of Henry VIII, being descended from the Yorkist monarch Edward IV through his mother Catherine, the sister of Elizabeth Woodville. Hated by the establishment, Elizabeth Woodville had been married to King Edward and like all of the Woodville's suffered in the wake of his death. Elizabeth was forced to seek the sanctuary of the church, other members of the family being summarily executed or murdered.

Buckingham's father had been one of those executed by Richard III and while he was still a young man Buckingham, Edward Stafford as he was then known, was disinherited and stripped of his position, rank and titles.

Fearful of Richard's wrath he had been forced to go into hiding in order to avoid a fate similar to his father's. It was something of a blessing for him when Henry Tudor landed in Wales to challenge the last of the Yorkist monarchs and finally eliminate Richard from the equation.

After Henry's victory at Bosworth Field in 1485 Stafford's titles had been restored to him but, despite gaining safety and a new lease of life from the Lancastrian dynasty, he harboured a deep resentment of the Tudors and their newfound positions of power. Even as an adolescent that bitter dislike was a significant element in his personality.

Following Bosworth, he had been made a ward of Margaret Beaufort, mother of Henry VII, but this did little to ease his anger. Indeed, closeness to Lady Margaret seemed only to increase his jealousy and bitterness. It was as if being in the same household as the Lancastrian 'mother of the clan' had brought home to him how much better things might have been if events had unfolded differently.

He may not have actually done anything more than vent his spleen in idle conversation but others certainly talked about Buckingham's claim to the throne:

Many spoke of my lorde of Buckingham, saying he was a noble man and wolde be a ryall ruler.[1]

'A noble man' and 'a ryall ruler' – that was language which Henry VIII was never able to ignore and despite his cousin's seeming acceptance of the status quo, from the beginning of his reign, Henry had Buckingham marked down as a potential problem.

Cardinal Wolsey, his dislike barely concealed, merely added his venom to Henry's concerns. Perhaps because of these worries, Buckingham was never a member of Henry's 'inner circle' and found himself being rebuked by the king on several occasions for things like failing to keep order within his lands along the Welsh Marches.

Buckingham's greatest weakness lay in his character. He was a weak and rather pompous individual who considered himself, socially and intellectually, totally superior to most people, even the king. In particular, he was vain and ever conscious of his looks and clothing. The gown he wore for the wedding of Prince Arthur, for example, was reputed to be worth over £1,000, an amazing sum for the time and guaranteed to up-stage the appearance of both of Arthur's royal parents.

He treated his own family very badly, particularly his brother Henry Stafford who had been flung into the Tower, almost as a surrogate prisoner on Buckingham's behalf, at the time of Henry's accession. On Stafford's release, Buckingham failed to endow his brother or give him land which would have ensured his financial independence but kept him on a leash as the manager of his estates.

Buckingham's tenants were treated equally as badly and were the victims of numerous enclosures of their rented and common land. Complaints and comments about the traditional rights of cottagers and farmers were repeatedly ignored by the duke who was totally convinced that he had almost a divine right to do as he wanted.

Buckingham's estates and holdings were sumptuous, in particular those at Penshurst Place and its adjacent lands close to Tonbridge in Kent. Here Buckingham hunted and entertained in lavish style, with no expense spared for his lucky guests.

It was perhaps unfortunate that Buckingham, as the senior noblemen in the kingdom, should become the mouthpiece of the great nobles, particularly those who resented their exclusion from high office in favour of men of low birth. There were plenty of those about!

Buckingham, along with most of the other nobles, hated Wolsey above any other official of the king. To the nobles, each of them schooled in the rights of their own line of descent and position in society, Wolsey was nothing more than a jumped-up commoner who had displaced them from their rightful position at the king's ear!

There was a story in common parlance at the time telling how the Cardinal had once dipped his fingers into a bowl of water which Buckingham was holding out for the king to wash his hands. Disgusted and unable to control himself Buckingham promptly poured the water over Wolsey's shoes. Whether or not there is any truth in the story it was the sort of behaviour of which the arrogant Buckingham was more than capable.

True or false, nobody did that type of thing to Thomas Wolsey and if he hadn't already earned the disapproval of the cardinal, the king's chief minister would have marked him down from that moment on. He would have been, had he but known it, a 'dead man walking'.

The Duke of Buckingham, having achieved his majority, became a significant if rather distant or peripheral figure in the court of Henry VIII. He was made Lord High Constable on Henry's accession in 1509 and was sufficiently well-regarded to be the bearer of the crown at the coronation of the new monarch. He duly became a Privy Councillor and in 1513 served as a Captain during the King's war with France. They were important positions but he was never 'close' to the king.

Despite his jealousy and envy of Henry VIII, Buckingham was one of the large contingent of English nobles to be present at the Field of Cloth of Gold in 1520 – and therefore seen as representing the king. He was in his element, parading around the enclosures in expensive clothes, drinking the nights away and gossiping with new friends and compatriots.

In fact, gossiping was one of the main causes of Buckingham's eventual downfall. Like all pompous and egotistical men, he had great difficulty in keeping his mouth closed. Discretion was never a part of his makeup and in the Tudor court, there were many who were happy to take advantage of this weakness.

As for his fall, it is more than possible that he was 'set up' by Wolsey. Certainly, the animosity between the two men was such that one or the other had to go and Wolsey was always the more vindictive of the pair.

All it took was a few words in Henry's ear, the sort of thing at which Wolsey was so efficient and to which the king was so susceptible. On 16 April 1521 Buckingham was summoned to court by Henry, an invitation that the duke could hardly refuse and there, swiftly and without warning, he was arrested and confined to the Tower of London. Henry's paranoia, more than probably fuelled by Wolsey's spleen, had struck again as there was little real reason for the duke's arrest.

The charges against him were confused and confusing, a web of indistinct information that was partly fact, partly fiction. They ranged from allegations that he had been heard discussing what would happen if Henry was to die unexpectedly to his strange and somewhat garbled wish that he could turn around and stick a knife into the king.

He was also supposed to have made ill-judged remarks about Henry's inability to father a male heir. Such information – perhaps stories might be a better description – could only have come from so-called acquaintances or friends.

They were the sort of remarks that might have been made during an evening of hard drinking or when relaxing after a day's hunting at Penshurst Place. They had little substance but they were undoubtedly ill-judged in a royal court that thrived on rumour and fear.

More significant, Buckingham had apparently engaged in conversation with one Nicholas Hopkins, a monk from the Carthusian Priory at Henton. Hopkins supposedly declared that he had been visited by a divine being. During the visitation, it had been revealed to him that one day Buckingham would 'have it all' – meaning, of course, the Crown of England and the title of king.[2]

Buckingham had apparently said nothing in reply to Hopkins's words but in Tudor England just listening to such remarks was considered treasonable. The prophecy was overheard by several of Buckingham's servants and passed on, under interrogation of course.

Wherever the stories originated the idea that it was the duke's loose tongue that caused his downfall not only lasted but grew. Ten years later Sir Thomas More, himself awaiting trial for supposed 'treason', was moved to write, warning his wife to declare herself to no one and even to be wary of to whom she listened. He used Buckingham as an example of how to get it wrong:

I think you have heard how the late Duke of Buckingham moved (was influenced by) with the fame of one that was reported for an (sic) holy monk and had much talking with him as after was a great part of his destruction and disheriting of his blood, and great slander and infamy of religion. It sufficeth me, good madam, to put you in remembrance of such things ... and the spirit of God shall keep you from talking with any persons of such manner.[3]

Buckingham was tried by seventeen of his peers, the court being presided over by the Duke of Norfolk. Henry himself examined the witnesses for the prosecution but Buckingham was not allowed the same privilege. Clearly, Henry had already made up his mind about the duke's guilt, not to mention his fate, and the case would not have been helped by 'needless' cross-examination of what were, anyway, fairly dubious witnesses.

A guilty verdict was inevitable and Buckingham was escorted to Tower Hill and executed on 17 May 1521. Hardly guilty of any serious sedition, it had been a tenuous prosecution that owed a great deal more to the king's paranoia than it did to justice.

Yet again, the trial and execution have to be considered in the context of the time. If Buckingham really had spoken to friends or colleagues about the inability of the king to procure an heir then it was foolish talk – and was more than enough to get him charged with treason. Even as early as 1520 the lack of a male heir was a major issue with the king and Buckingham should have known better.

In the political climate of the time, with Henry already beginning to look around for likely victims to feed his growing paranoia, it was proof positive of the duke's lack of common sense. And that, combined with Henry's growing worries and fears, was enough to send the unfortunate Duke of Buckingham to the block.

* * *

One of the few men to escape Henry's increasingly cruel subjugation of his nobles or, for that matter, his persecution of anyone who looked likely to become a threat, was Henry Stafford, Duke of Wiltshire. He had what was, in some respects, a lucky escape but things did not begin so precipitously for Stafford.

Stafford was the younger brother of the Duke of Buckingham and the son of Catherine Woodville. As already noted, he had spent the frenetic days of Henry's accession to the throne and subsequent coronation as a prisoner in the Tower. The thinking was that at least there, incarcerated in the country's greatest citadel, this Yorkist nobleman could cause little trouble.

Even so, it now seems to have been a strange precaution. Stafford was locked up while his brother the Duke of Buckingham, considerably more powerful and wealthy, was allowed to roam free and even take an active role in crowning the new monarch. In hindsight, it makes little sense but at the time Stafford was clearly considered a more likely threat. He was, at least, easier to get at!

Like his brother, Stafford had been a ward of Margaret Beaufort. There is no proof but Lady Margaret was relentless in her determination to place her son on the throne – and keep him there. In her old age, Margaret was as dynamic and driven as ever and it was more than possible that during his wardship Stafford would have been subjected to her Tudor propaganda. Possibly more significant, whatever opinions and ideas Lady Margaret heard from her two wards would have been illuminating.

If, during their childhood and adolescence, she had overheard the two Yorkist princes talking, one as indiscreet as the other, she would certainly have passed on the information to her son and his advisors. Servants would have been well-primed to listen for any anti-Tudor comment. Considering the characters of all those involved it is a distinct possibility.

Innocent, perhaps even misunderstood, Stafford was eventually released from the Tower without charge. There may have been no charge but a stain on his character there certainly was. The eternally suspicious Henry VIII ordered Wolsey to keep a close eye – a 'good watch' as he termed it – on Henry Stafford.

Working to the premise of keeping your friends close but your enemies even closer, Henry allowed Stafford to resume his former life at court. After a while, the king appeared to relent a little and Stafford even became something of a favourite of his.

Nobody quite knew what was in the king's mind but Stafford's love of hunting and eager participation in tournaments and jousting mirrored Henry's own interests and did seem to make him an ideal companion.

In 1513 Stafford was given command of one of Henry's ships during the war with France. It was hardly a significant position but, chained as he was to his brother's pocket book, Stafford had precious little to offer the king. He could certainly not pay for his commission.

He performed his duties adequately enough, however, and in due course had command of 500 soldiers during the siege of Therouanne. Henry later rewarded him by giving him several commissions in the west county and in September 1514 he was ordered, on behalf of the Crown, to investigate rural riots in Devon.

That same year he became a member of the Privy Council and, like his brother, was in attendance on the king at the Field of Cloth of Gold. It all cost money and by 1521 Stafford was in debt to the Crown for the sum of over £4,000. Despite appeals to his brother no money was forthcoming and the debt was left to build.

When Buckingham fell from Henry's favour in May 1521 Henry Stafford again came under suspicion. It is perhaps proof of the trumped-up charges against Buckingham that nothing was ever done to arrest or persecute Stafford.

Meanwhile, the 'watch' was still in place and there can be little doubt that Henry Stafford would have been close to the top of the king's 'hit list'. It could only be a matter of time before Henry began to move against him.

Stafford served with the army one last time, crossing to France in August 1522. However, he forestalled any action on the king's part by dying in April 1522. He died without heirs and his title of Duke of Wiltshire was promptly granted to Thomas Boleyn, father of Henry's second wife.

It had been an uneasy, unproductive life but at least he had avoided the fate of his brother and so many more. It was not an accolade that was easily achieved in Tudor Britain.

* * *

Sir Thomas More has been fixed in popular imagination by the play and film *A Man for All Seasons* where he is portrayed as a saintly, God-fearing martyr, his character contrasting beautifully with Thomas Cromwell as the vacillating, two-faced bureaucrat. There are elements of truth in the description of More – and Cromwell too, come to that – but, perhaps more importantly Sir Thomas is shown as a victim of the furious temper and deeply rooted paranoia of the king.

Born in London, his father a lawyer and judge, Thomas More became a household page to John Morton who was Archbishop of Canterbury and Chancellor of England under Henry VII in the early 1490s. Educated at Oxford and trained to be a lawyer, Thomas More was intensely religious and for a while even considered a career in the church. Eventually, he decided against this step but retained his strong religious beliefs.

To the end of his life those beliefs were so intense, so deeply felt, that he wore a hair shirt beneath his ordinary clothes and often indulged in self-flagellation. Despite his reactionary views on religion, he was unusual in that he believed in education for all and brought up his children, in particular his daughter Margaret, to be free-thinking and widely schooled individuals.

Thomas More practised law in the city but in 1504 entered Parliament as a member, a role that he relished and where he enjoyed success. He duly came to the notice of Cardinal Wolsey. He made a number of diplomatic missions with the Lord Chancellor and in 1523, on the cardinal's recommendation, was rewarded with the post of Speaker in the House of Commons.

In due course, he became friendly with the king who appreciated his wit and learning and marked him down as a useful ally. In 1529 Thomas More succeeded to the office of Lord Chancellor after Wolsey's fall from grace.

During his time as Chancellor, the reactionary More was adamantly opposed to the Reformation that was taking place in Europe. He saw Martin Luther, Ulrich Zwingli, John Calvin and other reformers as heretics and was determined to prevent their beliefs taking root in England. He happily suppressed Tyndale's English translation of the New Testament and, during his short time as Chancellor, sentenced six would-be reformers to be burned at the stake.

It was inevitable that, sooner or later, his fervent beliefs would bring him into conflict with his friend the king. They quarrelled first over the issue of what defined heresy and the new heresy laws but it was Henry's 1534 Act of Supremacy that finally proved to be a step too far for Sir Thomas.

The Act of Supremacy, which effectively made Henry Head of the Church in England, contradicted all of More's beliefs and, holding fast to the concept of Papal Supremacy, he refused to sign the accompanying oath. This oath required the signature of all men of substance, officially anointing Henry as the Supreme Head of the Church in England. Refusal to sign it was a treasonous stance. In the case of Sir Thomas More his refusal to sign totally infuriated the king.

More was not alone in his opposition to the Act of Supremacy but together with John Fisher, Bishop of Rochester, he was certainly the most renowned and best-known refuser. It meant that a collision between the king and his former friend had now been made inevitable.

Under huge pressure, Sir Thomas eventually allowed that Henry could, if he chose, declare himself the supreme leader of the English Church but he still refused to sign the oath because it included a statement against the Pope. Such an acknowledgement would therefore violate his conscience. To Sir Thomas More that conscience was central to his existence, believing that it was the voice of God operating within him and within all men.

Henry was further upset and bitterly hurt when his old friend refused to acknowledge the annulment of his marriage to Catherine of Aragon. When Sir Thomas duly refused to attend the coronation of Anne Boleyn, Henry took it very personally.

Henry saw More's absence at the ceremony as a snub and a betrayal of their friendship. Nobody snubbed the king and his friendship, once broken or cast aside, could never be regained. Anger and paranoia mixing freely together, the king set Thomas Cromwell the task of ridding the country of Sir Thomas More.

What followed was a complex and 'dirty' business. To begin with, More, who had resigned as Chancellor in May 1532, was accused of accepting bribes during his time in office. The accusations were ludicrous and quickly dismissed but it was only the start of the campaign.

Much more significant was the charge that he had conspired with Elizabeth Barton, the so-called *Maid of Kent*, whose anti-Reformation/anti-annulment views had already brought her into conflict with the king. It was dangerous ground for a man like Thomas More who was so violently opposed to any sort of break with Rome.

More had, indeed, met with Barton, as had the king, Cardinal Wolsey and Bishop Fisher. Yet while acknowledging the validity of many of her opinions, Sir Thomas had wisely advised her to stay out of the Crown's business. As far as he was concerned there was no charge to answer. The

Lords and Members of Parliament listening to the charges agreed and the matter was dropped.

Cromwell was not about to let More off the hook, however. Called before a commission formed in April 1534 to investigate his beliefs, Thomas More found himself in a perilous position. His freedom and his life depended on the findings of the commission and the members were all either Cromwell's men or totally dependent on the king for their livelihood.

Faced with the dilemma of what to do and say, More finally accepted that Parliament may well have had the right to declare that Anne Boleyn was indeed Queen of England. It was a significant admission. However, he refused to acknowledge the declaration's spiritual validity. Nobody had the right to question God's laws and the jurisdiction of his representative on earth. Arrest on charges of treason inevitably followed.

Confined to the Tower, Thomas More spent many months in captivity, denied access to books and to decent food. His family was forbidden to visit and he lived out the months in quiet contemplation that was neither fulfilling nor helpful to his physical health.

Thomas More lived in squalid surroundings and when the moment of his execution finally arrived, he could barely walk. He had to be assisted to the block on Tower Hill. He went to his death on 16 July 1535 with courage, believing to the end that he had done the right thing:

> Going to the scaffold, Thomas More was so weak and ready to fall that he said merrily to Walsingham (lieutenant of the Tower) "I pray you, Master Lieutenant, see me safe up and for my coming down, let me shift for myself."[4]

Henry was later to regret the death of Thomas More. It was one more friend he could no longer call on for advice or engage in conversation on an equal footing. A humanist and writer of some note, More's *Utopia* is still regarded as a work of great beauty and skill. Henry might even have had a part in its writing and publication.

However, Sir Thomas had committed the supreme mistake of standing in opposition to a man with the power to crush him without a moment's consideration.

In the battle of conscience versus the temporal power of someone rapidly on the way to becoming a tyrant worthy of the old Roman emperors, there could only ever be one winner – at least on this earth.

Sir Thomas More went to his death convinced that his soul had been saved. Henry had dealt with his troublesome friend in the manner of a small boy happily and mindlessly pulling the wings off flies and other insects!

*   *   *

In Thomas Cromwell, the king had, perhaps unexpectedly, discovered the man who would give him exactly what he wanted, at least until his usefulness expired. And as the years unfolded those 'wants' grew increasingly significant.

Cromwell was born in Putney, the son of a blacksmith and cloth merchant. He was, by his own admission, something of a ruffian in his youth, leaving a brutal family environment where he was regularly beaten by his drunken father to live for a while on the streets.

The streets of London were a temporary refuge and he soon headed for France where he may well have become a mercenary soldier in the service of the French king. He had more in mind, however, than playing the part of just another simple soldier

Soldier or not, what is certain is that Cromwell spent time in Italy, probably with the military but at the same time gaining a clear understanding of diplomacy and the traditional money markets. He knew Rome reasonably well, court and back streets alike, but by 1515 he was back in London where he married and began to make his way in the world of local politics.

In 1517 and 1518 he led embassies to Pope Leo X asking for the reinstatement of indulgences for the town of Boston in Lincolnshire. By 1520 he was well established and happily moving in mercantile and legal circles. Three years later, as a burgess, Thomas Cromwell took a seat in the House of Commons.

In 1524 Cromwell joined the household staff of the Lord Chancellor, Thomas Wolsey. He maintained his legal practice, having been elected a member of Greys Inn, but when Wolsey appointed him a member of his Council his career took a giant leap forward.

Both Wolsey and Henry recognised Cromwell's abilities as a 'fixer' and as someone who was not unduly worried by too many scruples or principles. He increasingly came to be indispensable to the king as Wolsey was shunted sideways and finally, being unable to procure the divorce that Henry wanted, dispensed with altogether.

Cromwell was well aware of Henry's volatile personality and by the time of Wolsey's fall from grace he had seen the king's temper in action on a regular basis. He had already fallen foul of the king's anger himself on more than a few occasions, being punched and slapped across the head by the furious monarch. Thomas Cromwell would have killed lesser men for such insults.

He was ambitious, however, and was clear that the only way to power and prestige for a man like himself lay in doing exactly what the king wanted. If that involved unpleasant moments, so be it. He knew that he was going to do exactly what Henry wanted.

Thomas Cromwell was perhaps the most significant and able of all of Henry's many advisors and councillors. Hard-working, gifted, not above looking for the main chance – particularly for himself – he was a supremely significant civil servant, a man without scruples operating in the reign of a man equally as self-interested. It was just unfortunate that the other man happened to be king.

Without someone like Thomas Cromwell, it is doubtful if many of the developments and changes of Henry's reign could ever have happened. So, too, for the troubles and disturbances that lay ahead.

Chapter Five

Riot, Unrest and the Occasional Brawl

Throughout Henry's reign, just as there had been for many years before he became king, social banditry thrived in the more rural parts of the country. The most obvious example of this banditry was poaching.

Poaching was particularly prevalent in times of hardship, when the harvest was poor, when the weather was bad and, as a consequence, when the year's crop failed. Yet the crime was not confined just to hard times. Poaching was almost a leisure activity in many parts of the country, areas like Hampshire, Cornwall and the Welsh Marches where game was plentiful and outbreaks occurred on a regular basis, particularly between the years 1513 and 1525.

If poaching took place at night, it was technically a capital offence, something that had more to do with illicit and potentially rebellious gatherings in the hours of darkness than it ever did with hunting deer or other animals. In such cases the king's justice was swift and the night-poachers were invariably despatched with a minimum degree of fuss.

Taking the king's or noblemen's deer during daylight hours was a different matter. Daylight poaching was considered a lesser offence. It was not exactly tolerated but on many occasions those in charge of regions where offences took place were happy to turn a blind eye to the practice, seeing it as part of the normal activities of the peasant population who needed the occasional hunk of meat to keep strong and fit. Apart from anything else it also helped sharpen their archery skills!

The folk tales of Robin Hood and his band of outlaws were hugely popular at this time, the populace, landowners and peasants alike, seeing no discrepancy between the legend and the fact. Even the king enjoyed and participated in the legend of the 'poaching outlaws'.

On May Day 1515 he and Catherine of Aragon were entertained by 200 green coated 'outlaws' and Henry himself dressed totally in green livery for the occasion. A skilful and hard-fought archery contest was followed by a traditional poacher's breakfast of stolen venison. Henry and his wife were thoroughly entertained and showed no disquiet, happily tucking into the 'poached' goodies.[1]

Only rarely did activities such as poaching result in an upsurge of riot and affray. However, there were other nefarious activities, other occasions when matters did get out of hand and then they required the attention of those in authority. Very often these outbreaks were centred on standards of living for the peasantry, particularly on issues such as the reduction of wages.

Above all, there was the issue of enclosures. A rapid increase in the population during the first quarter of the century had made the provision of food supplies for the populace a critical problem that needed to be solved, and solved quickly. As far as the landowners were concerned, one obvious solution was to implement a system of enclosures.

Enclosing land – literally turning previously wide-open hills and fields into smaller enclaves fenced in like stockades – might answer some of the problems but it was a hugely emotive area. To the great landowners of England, enclosures solved all of their difficulties, making their land more profitable and cutting down on expenditure, but for the peasantry, it was a process that trampled on their rights and their traditional way of life.

The benefits were easy to see. Supplies of corn and meat could be greatly increased by the all year round use of enclosed land – and, of course, that meant huge profits for the landowners. It was the issue of sheep that caused most problems. Large flocks of sheep could graze on the short grass of the enclosed pastures while, at the same time, corn could be grown and harvested in other fields protected by fences or hedges. And the benefits of enclosing did not lie just with the easy provision of food.

The early sixteenth century also saw an enormous increase in the demand for wool. Prices rose dramatically, something which made the process of gathering together a few thousand sheep almost an economic necessity. Inevitably, of course, it impacted on the peasant farmers who had traditionally tilled the earth in what was little more than subsistence farming.

Sheep farming needed relatively few workers, perhaps just one or two men to guard the flock and a few more casual participants to help out at lambing time. The rest of the village population was suddenly out of work. Tenant farmers were thrown off their holdings as arable farming decreased by as much as twenty or even thirty per cent.

Matters might have been more acceptable to the small farmers if had been just the huge manorial estates that were being enclosed. Common land, traditionally available for the peasants to farm or graze their few animals as well as providing areas to hunt for rabbits and hares, was also enclosed. Like a criss-cross of military fortifications over the land, hedges were planted and grown, ditches were dug and gates erected, thereby prohibiting access to everyone but the Lord of the Manor and his few workers.

There was, inevitably, a reaction to this dramatic and sudden change in farming style. Moving from arable to sheep farming might have seemed simple to the landowning gentry but to the peasants and small tenant farmers, it was a life-changing process.

The reaction took the form of anti-enclosure riots when gangs of frustrated peasants took the law into their own hands and set about destroying the hated symbols of enclosures. Almost gleefully, gates were burned, hedges cut down and ditches filled in. Most of these episodes were small-scale affairs, involving at most one or possibly two villages, and were dealt with at a local level by the landowner and his men – a flogging or two and the occasional tenant turned out of his house. Very rarely was the punishment anything more serious.

Only rarely did the riots warrant outside intervention. That usually happened when the protests and subsequent riots centred on market towns or trade centres. Nottingham was hit twice by enclosure riots, in 1511 and again in 1512 while Gloucester suffered severe outbreaks in 1513. Southampton saw several riots in the years after 1517 and even London was subjected to outbreaks of disorder and complaints about enclosures in the years following 1518.

In the more rural parts of the kingdom the nobles who owned the land on which the peasants lived and worked, held what really were powers of life and death over their tenants. In matters of law breaking or failure to toe the line, those nobles assumed the roles of sheriff, judge, jury and executioner all in one.

Communication between the capital and the more distant parts of the realm was tenuous in the extreme. It might not have been an ideal situation but London and the central authority of the king were days, sometimes even weeks, away from areas like Yorkshire and Cornwall. Support or even advice from the centre were rarely forthcoming with the result that the men on the spot were expected to hold and use the authority given to them by the monarch.

The great noblemen of England were generally responsible for the safety and control of a county or a shire – a 'country' as it was termed – while the lesser nobles had oversight of groups of villages or towns. It was a hierarchical system, the last vestiges of feudalism, but it seemed to work, at least in times of plenty.

It remains difficult to know quite how many local riots and disturbances actually took place during Henry's reign. This is mainly because very few of the local nobles, the men who were formally charged by the king with maintaining the peace, ever kept accurate records. They had a vested interest in keeping quiet about disturbances in their area. Too many riots, too much acting out by the locals, would reflect badly on their ability to keep order and so documentary evidence of what went on remains severely limited.

When serious disturbances occurred, as they did in Cornwall and Devon in the early days of the reign, the local nobleman would call a muster. This was a gathering of men, armed with their traditional long bows and wearing whatever protective clothing they possessed, who came together with the specific purpose of putting down the riots.

It was something like the assembly of a local defence force or an early form of Home Guard, a gathering which could and often did last for several weeks. Men were entitled to be paid for answering the call, a factor that took the edge off having to arrest or maybe even kill men who they knew and had perhaps stood alongside them at the previous muster.

Most of the disturbances were restricted to fairly small or local areas. Anything else was a much more significant event and that would probably require the intervention of the king and the troops of some noble baron. That was when riot morphed into rebellion – as we shall see.

Avoiding such riots and uprisings was the main reason behind the Tudor use of the annual summer progresses. Henry VIII got it down to a fine art, spending most summers – at least when he was young and fit enough – out on the road, keeping his subjects happy and less inclined to complain:

In 1535 he visited Gloucestershire and the Bristol Channel, Salisbury, Winchester and Southampton. This particular progress may well have prevented rebellion in the religiously conservative South West of England. In 1536 the South West, which had received a visit from Henry, did not rise up in rebellion but the North of England, which he had neglected, rose up in the most serious rebellion of his reign.[2]

There was an extra, more pragmatic aim behind each summer progress. It also enabled the king and his court to escape the disease-ridden capital for a few months when the stink of refuse and animal waste were unbearable and the likelihood of catching some ailment was at its highest.

Henry was something of a hypochondriac and was constantly ordering the houses and palaces where he stayed to be fumigated with smoke and substances like vinegar. Keeping on the move was one of his cures for any ailment like the plague or sweating sickness.

Servants would be sent ahead of the royal party to fumigate and clean the house where the king would stay. It was an exhausting but well-planned process that sometimes seemed to go on forever. During his progress of 1535, he visited no fewer than thirty royal residences plus numerous grand houses in a period of four months. A moving target, clearly, was more difficult to hit!

*   *   *

It was not just the rural areas where discontent was liable to flare up. The city of London was not exempt from riot and disturbance. The mood of the street mobs in the city was always difficult to assess and the London apprentices, a powerful and influential factor in controlling the capital, were nothing if not volatile and aggressive. The most serious outbreak of rioting in London took place in the spring of 1517 and became known as Evil May Day.

At the beginning of the sixteenth century, London was already a diverse and multi-cultural city with approximately 3,000 foreign immigrants living there. That amounted to 6% of the city's total population, many of the immigrants coming from France, Italy and Germany but the vast majority being wool workers and artisans from the Low Countries.[3]

Resentment had been simmering for some time, Londoners being unhappy with the large number of foreigners resident in their city. They called them 'strangers', a derogatory term that caught the mood of the moment and emphasised the difference between native-born English citizens and the newcomers.

In complaints since heard many times, Londoners screamed that the 'strangers', who had been encouraged to settle in England to aid the economy, were taking their jobs, using and abusing the scant social resources of the native-born Englanders. They bought or rented quality accommodation and were renowned for buying up scant food supplies. Anger was abroad and hostility was hovering close to the surface.

The writer and chronicler Edward Hall was in London at the time and carefully recorded his emotions along with making a record of the attitudes and behaviour of the citizens. A lawyer by profession, Hall recorded the sights that he witnessed both in the lead up to Evil May Day and on the day itself. His chronicle of the event was unashamedly partisan, taking the side of the average Londoner:

> The multitude of strangers was so great about London that the poor English artificers could scarce get any living, and most of all the strangers were so proud that they disdained, mocked and oppressed the Englishmen.[4]

Matters came to a head on May Day 1517 when a series of serious riots broke out across the city. They had been preceded by an inflammatory and xenophobic speech made two weeks before by a preacher called Dr Bell (or Dr Beal in some accounts). He gave his talk at St Paul's Cross, a public site available to all, and which invariably attracted crowds of many hundreds to listen to the words of the preachers and public speakers.

The address given by Bell was particularly well attended and brought screams of delight and agreement from the listeners. The 'strangers', according to Edward Hall, simply passed off the sermon as empty rhetoric:

> Of this sermon many a light person took courage and openly spoke against strangers … The Genevese, the Frenchmen and other strangers said and boasted themselves to be in such favour with the king and his council that they met nought by the rulers of the city.[5]

Dr Bell's invective was hugely effective but he was just the mouthpiece for the anti-stranger's group, the real instigator being a London broker and second-hand dealer, a renowned hater and opponent of all 'strangers' or in-comers. His name was John Lincoln.

Just a few days before, Lincoln had nailed a letter to the door of St Paul's, a common practice for those who felt they had something to say. It was a vitriolic piece of writing, condemning the government and those in power for encouraging the 'strangers' to come and make their homes in London. However, in an age of illiteracy and poor reading skills, it had only minimal results. What was needed was a public address – enter Dr Bell.

Encouraged by Lincoln, in his speech Bell called on all Englishmen 'to cherish and defend themselves and to hurt and grieve aliens for the common weal'.[6] It was fiery stuff that inflamed the passions of the mob and, in particular, the London apprentices who were always ready for a little excitement, particularly if it involved violence and aggression.

For the two weeks leading up to May Day 1517, as John Lincoln sat back to watch his work come to a climax, there were sporadic attacks on foreigners. Many of the victims were hospitalised and several attackers locked up in gaol to await trial. The city was alive, boiling and rancid with rumour:

> Then suddenly there was a common secret rumour, and no man could tell how it began, that on May Day next, the city would rebel and slay all the aliens.[7]

The idea that on the great day itself the population would rise up and massacre the 'strangers' had a delicious appeal to many of the citizens of London, no matter how peaceful and law-abiding they might normally be. The authorities panicked and on the evening of 30 April, the aldermen and mayor announced that they were implementing a curfew at 9.00pm that night. As it was already 8.30 the announcement brought shock and, more significantly, anger to the populace.

The immediate result was that many young apprentices defied the order and began gathering together in small but threatening groups. A local alderman, John Mundy, approached one group and ordered them to disperse. The gang rounded on him and, in fear of his life, Mundy fled. It was a signal for general unrest and within the hour over 1,000 apprentices and other angry citizens had congregated in Cheapside.

Mob-handed, they broke into Newgate Prison and freed some of the individuals arrested for attacking foreigners during the previous fortnight. They then moved, en masse, to St Martin le Grand to the north of St Paul's where many of the 'strangers' lived.

There they were met by the redoubtable Sir Thomas More, acting in his capacity as Under-Sheriff of London. Sir Thomas spoke to the crowd and managed to calm them but, unfortunately, before they could disperse the panic-stricken residents of the area began to hurl stones, sticks, even boiling water, at the crowd.

It totally undermined More's attempt to disperse the protesters and the result was an eruption of violence. It came with a ferocity rarely seen in the city. Houses were broken into, windows smashed and wholesale looting of the richer properties began. For several hours the mob ran unchecked through the streets and the flames of burning houses lit up the night sky:

> Then all the misruled persons ranne to the dores and wyndowes of saynct Martyn and spoyled all that they found and cast it into the strete, and lefte few houses unspoiled.[8]

Henry, sleeping peacefully in his palace at Richmond, was woken and informed of the situation. He immediately ordered the Duke of Norfolk to bring his retainers into the city and put down the riot. Norfolk reacted swiftly and despite the rioters barring the gates of the city, he was soon in the streets of London with 1,300 troops.

The soldier's response to the groups of rioters was brutal, resulting in many broken heads, but it was also hugely effective. Most of the rioters fled before their attacks. Even so, despite their efforts, there were still moments of panic.

Sir Richard Cholmeley, Lieutenant of the Tower, was so frightened that he ordered the firing of several artillery pieces housed in the fortress. The cannon shots had no effect on the rioters but they did cause damage to private property with the result that the city elders later made a complaint to the Crown. In general, however, Norfolk's presence was enough to quieten things down and by 4.00am all was calm.

It is unclear if any deaths were occasioned during the rioting. Hall declares not but it is unlikely that brawling and fighting on such a level did not lead to at least some fatalities.

Over 300 rioters were arrested and flung into gaol. Most of them were soon pardoned, Henry staging a hugely effective piece of play-acting where he allowed himself to be implored by Queen Catherine and Wolsey. Together, they begged the king to show clemency. The frightened apprentices shouted and screamed their thanks and the king's stock went up tenfold.

There were casualties, however. Thirteen of the more serious offenders were convicted of treason and executed on 4 May. John Lincoln, instigator of the riots, followed them to the scaffold three days later. His final words were the sign of a totally unrepentant man – 'You know I did it for your own good.'

*   *   *

Evil May Day had been a dangerous time, a riot that could easily have escalated into open rebellion. Henry's pardoning of the rioters had been a deliberate ploy, designed to take the heat out of what was a great deal more than a mere show of unhappiness from the residents of London. It was a brilliant performance from Henry who appeared at his most benevolent and generous.

There were reasons for his attitude. It was common knowledge that the king had a considerable vested interest in maintaining the presence of the 'strangers' in his city. And that was hardly the message he wanted to give to his subjects. Cloak it, keep it hidden, even if it was an open secret amongst the people of London.

In return for valuable satin and silks at very low prices – or even as gifts – the king had given many of the richer 'strangers' all manner of privileges. These ranged from tax-free concessions to trading rights and hospitality at court. Two men, in particular, were recipients of these special deals. Francesco de Bardi was a Florentine merchant while Frenchman Jean Meautys was one of the king's long-term private secretaries.

Like Bardi, Meautys had made his home in London, forging a career for himself during delicate negotiations between Henry and the French government in the early part of the reign. Henry kept him on after his initial success, the Frenchman becoming a regular attendee at court.

Meautys lived in great style in a large house called Green Gate, on Leadenhall Street where it was commonly alleged that he kept open house for all manner of French criminals, pickpockets and the like. The house was supposed by the London crowds to be outside the law.

Bardi was a particular favourite of the king, regularly supplying Henry and members of the court with all manner of luxurious goods. In 1513, in return for his 'gifts', Henry granted him the right to trade both in Britain and overseas without having to pay customs duties.

Francesco de Bardi enjoyed an elite status and an extravagant lifestyle. However, his arrogant and scandalous behaviour infuriated many of those who encountered him – or even those who didn't but simply knew of him by reputation.

Bardi's behaviour was indeed shocking. A great womaniser, he once persuaded the wife of an English acquaintance to come and live with him. She brought with her all of her husband's silver and gold plate but as if that was not enough Bardi then sued the abandoned husband for failing to pay the cost of his wife's lodgings – and won the case.

Such behaviour, while not excusing the riot, did not endear the 'strangers' to the mob. Bardi and Meautys, along with other lesser-known foreign merchants and citizens, promptly became targets for the rioters. Both of their houses were ransacked, their possessions stolen. The crowd did attempt to capture the two men but Bardi and Meautys were ahead of them and made off to safety as soon as the riots began.

When the rioters moved on to the area known as Blanchappleton where many of the foreign cobblers and shoemakers lived – ordinary, hardworking citizens, not rich merchants or courtiers – they contented themselves with breaking into the houses and throwing the shoes into the streets. The pavements and roadways were soon littered with expensive footwear. From there the locals were happy to help themselves to more than a few new pairs of shoes each, ready for the coming winter season.

* * *

Life in Henry's England could be parlous in the extreme, even for the most law-abiding of citizens. In an age when clean water was scarce, the common drink was ale with the result that drunkenness was common. Every village had its tavern, usually just the front room of the landlord's house and everyone had access to a weapon of some description, be it a simple bill hook or an ancient sword or dagger. It did not take much for ale or beer induced anger to flare up.

With a population of just two million at the start of his reign, rising rapidly over the course of the next thirty years to approximately four million, the homicide rate was five times that of today. However, the isolated nature of many rural communities meant that a large number of the murders were put down to other reasons – suicide and death from natural causes – or more often simply left unresolved.

There were no police to investigate, monitor and control behaviour and while some larger communities might have a village constable it was normally left up to the citizens to apprehend villains and give justice. Life or death? It was something of a lottery.

Despite the lack of a police force, justice was meted out on a clearly defined basis. This could range from a whipping or a period of time locked into the village stocks to the cutting off of a hand for theft. Cucking or ducking stools were regularly used as were the village 'scolds', iron masks placed over the heads of subversive individuals. Most of the victims of the 'scolds' were women whose gossip, it was felt, could easily undermine the social order and destroy reputations.

Branding, usually on the forehead or chest, or the cutting off of ears were other brutal but deliberately obvious punishments, the idea being to display or expose the victims to the public as the criminals they had been proven to be. Every town or village had its whipping post and its pillory, all of them well-used.[9]

Certain groups and individuals were often singled out for abuse. Beggars and vagrants were an obvious target. These were rootless men or women who roamed the countryside and were particularly feared for a number of reasons.

In an age when everyone was supposed to come under the control of their social superiors, these wandering vagabonds owed allegiance to no one. That made them a distinct threat to the social order, if only in the minds of those in authority.

Not only that, being free to roam wherever they wanted, beggars and vagrants could pass on rumours and ideas that the government, local and national, did not want to see spread. It was surreptitious and it was beyond the control of government officials – therefore it was dangerous.

The potential for such vagrants and beggars to cause violence was a constant fear for the villagers and townsfolk of Tudor England. Along with fear of being abused by gypsies, threats of what the beggars and vagrants might do were often used to quell bad behaviour in children and make them go quietly to bed at night.

This was particularly the case when the beggars came in bands, as sometimes happened. Small wonder that the nursery rhyme, dating to Henry's reign, created such a frisson of fear in remote and distant hamlets:

> Hark, hark, dogs do bark,
> Beggars are coming to town.
> Some in rags, some in jags
> And one in a velvet gown.[10]

The word 'jags' refers to an opening or gash in the arm of a tunic, usually in the shape of a diamond, which overlayed a different colour cloth beneath. It was a style of dress that was much in fashion during the early sixteenth century, thus dating the rhyme to Henry's time on the throne. What is now regarded as a child's nursery rhyme sums up the terror caused by the coming of the beggars.

There was an erroneous assumption that while jobs were available – which they were not – beggars and vagrants simply did not want to work. Therefore, in the main, they were met by and dealt with a total lack of compassion. Their welcome to a village or town was one of violence.

The Poor Law Act of 1531 ordered that any beggars found wandering should be whipped and then sent back to their home parish where they were known and might – and the word was *might* – receive help and sustenance.

Under the Vagrancy Act of 1547, a vagrant was defined as any able-bodied man or woman who had been three days without a master or out of employment. Even a first offence led to the letter V being branded on the victim's chest and later offences could see the vagrant being forced to work as a slave to the man who had denounced him for two years or more.[11]

In a world where poverty was caused largely by the rapid and unexpected growth in population the vagrancy laws were harsh and Henry's dissolution of the monasteries – the only places where the vagrants might receive help or shelter – was to cause even more hardship for the poor.

In the years following Henry's death, less stringent rules and regulations were introduced. Even so, by modern standards treatment of vagrants remained relatively harsh up until the middle of the twentieth century.

*   *   *

Women, although regarded by law as being totally subservient to their husbands, were often to be found at the front of rioting groups. It was, perhaps, the ideal opportunity to 'let off steam', to actually influence events as they unfolded. More often it was simply that emotion took over and the repressed nature of women exploded into vicious outbursts of violence.

On occasions, mobs were made up of women alone. At such times their fury was a terrible thing to see and many men quailed before their anger. Only very rarely were mobs of women prosecuted en masse – Tudor sensibilities went only so far. Realising this, there were apparently times when men disguised themselves as women in order to take part in the demonstration. Mostly, however, the women were left to their own devices to implement direct action.

In 1517, in the area of Windsor and Eton, such 'direct action' was directed at one individual when a group of women fell foul of what can only be described as mass hysteria. For some reason they became suspicious of one of their number, an unmarried woman by the name of Alice Riding who had, they believed, recently been pregnant.

Several dozen of the outraged local women seized Alice and stripped her. After examining her naked body, it was agreed that she had indeed recently given birth. Abuse of Alice Riding went no further but it was later revealed that her baby – fathered by a local priest – had died and been buried in an orchard in the area.[12]

Even Anne Boleyn, never popular at the best of times, once came close to abuse at the hands of a baying group of women. In October 1531, learning that Anne was dining, without guards or soldiers, at a house close to the Thames, a mob of local women quickly gathered.

The mob grew rapidly in size and strength as more and more women saw a chance to let people know exactly what they felt about 'the goggle-eyed whore of the king', as they called Anne. In their hundreds, they went streaming out of the city to join the original protesters. Soon, close to 7,000 screaming harpies had arrived in front of the house where Queen Anne, without the protection and presence of the king, was dining.

Anne was alerted to her danger and managed to escape before the mob broke in. There seems to have been no retribution exacted as the mob, learning that their target had fled, quickly withered away and headed back home.

Other protests against Anne Boleyn tended to be individual actions rather than group gatherings. It was far easier to deal with individuals than with groups so that when the wife of a London goldsmith was overheard calling the queen's father a bawd 'to his wife and both his daughters' she was immediately arrested and sent to prison. She was one of many so punished.[13]

* * *

Minority groupings had no place in Tudor England and Wales. Henry and his advisors were intent on establishing a strong central government with the king and Parliament firmly in control. This was a major development as until then Parliament and the way it had been used by medieval monarchs had been a mere cypher.

Minority groups were seen as a distinct threat to the status quo. Even then Henry was more than capable of playing a double-handed game and using whatever means he could to lay his hands on money to fund his lifestyle.

Jews had been expelled from England by Edward I in 1290 but despite the stringent application of the law, small gatherings of Jewish people did manage to remain in the country. They were mainly secret groups, members keeping their faith and traditions well hidden. By 1550 there were approximately 100 of them living in the London area alone.

As he had done with the 'strangers', Henry unashamedly used the Jewish bankers and money brokers for both personal and state finances. To sustain this, he happily turned a blind eye to their illegal presence in his country.

The king even went so far as to defend the Jewish banker Diago Mendes, a renowned figure who traded in both London and Antwerp. Mendes had been accused of attempting to create a Jewish enclave in England but Henry's intervention prevented him from being prosecuted.

Eventually, however, the king was obliged to break up the Jewish groups when antisemitic factions within his court and in the country generally began to complain about the presence of what was termed 'Christ-killers.' A strong strain of antisemitism, fuelled in many respects by the Crusades – despite the last one having been launched many years before – ran through Tudor England and, unlike the king and his court, the ordinary people of Henry's dominion could see little or no benefit from the presence of the Jews.

It was a potentially difficult situation that saw Henry caught between two prongs. He had no wish to annoy either the Jewish financiers or his courtiers. In the end, he decided on discretion and the members of the secret Jewish groups were exiled from England.

It was a bitter and discordant blow for most of the families who had made the country their home for many years. Hardly a pogrom in the accepted sense of the word, this further displacement of the English Jews was still a cruel and unfeeling gesture on behalf of the crown.

It was not in the character of the Jews to rebel or riot at the king's ruling but the hurt was plain to see as they shuffled onto ships in the Port of London to make their new homes on the Continent. Not until the time of Oliver Cromwell's Commonwealth were Jewish people allowed to reside and work once more in England and Wales.

It remains one of the interesting facts about Henry's reign that there were probably fewer uprisings or revolts than there could or maybe should have been. That may sound disingenuous but when looking back at some of the events which occurred the potential that they held for trouble was vast. It remains surprising that there were not far more serious incidents.

The 1536 Act of Union which united England and Wales is one example. The Act contained a specific ruling which has now become infamous in Wales. The Welsh language clause banned all monoglot Welsh speakers from holding public office, relegating the natural language of the country to purely social activities. As a result, English became the sole language for the ruling classes in Wales.

Since the conquest of Wales by Edward I, the Welsh nation had been fighting, both directly and more surreptitiously, for independence. The fifteenth century with the rebellion of Owain Glyndwr had been a particularly difficult period for English monarchs like Henry IV and his successor, Henry V. Arguably, the hills and valleys of Wales were instrumental in giving Henry V his military training, skills which he went on to put to good purpose in France during the Agincourt campaign.

Throughout the century anti-Welsh feelings had been rife, particularly in the border regions and in the capital, with English workers using the age-old adage that the Welsh, unable to make a living in their own country, were crossing Offa's Dyke to take the jobs of the English. There was an element of truth in the complaint but that did not make the resentment of the Welsh, who endured insults, beatings and riots, any less bitter.

Henry VIII's Act of Union had little to do with soothing Welsh hurt but was part and parcel of his desire to see control vested in a strong central government or authority. Similarly, there was no great desire to destroy the Welsh language. The system of law and administration was another matter. Even after the Edwardian conquest of the country Wales had always had its own legal code – not any longer:

> Its (the Acts) purpose was, with the introduction of uniformity in the legal codes of England and Wales to have uniformity also in their administration ... Nevertheless the consequences of the stipulations with regard to language were deplorable.[14]

Quite possibly the accession of Henry VII with his clear Welsh antecedents had helped the situation but it remains a puzzle as to why the people of Wales accepted the situation so readily. They had spent hundreds of years kicking at the control of the English overlords, now they seemed happy to just roll over and accept the situation and their position as second-class citizens. It was to be another few hundred years before the first signs of Welsh nationalism really began to emerge.

In an age of slavery and oppression, it was rare for people of colour to be seen in England and Wales but that did not mean there were no black people in the country.

Queen Catherine of Aragon brought with her Catalina de Cardones, a black attendant and lady-in-waiting, when she first came to the country in 1501, prior to her wedding with Prince Arthur. Catalina stayed with the queen for many years, a popular and well-respected figure in the royal court.

There were other black faces at court, notably the trumpeter John Blacke who served both Henry VII and Henry VIII until 1512 – and was paid more than double the wage of farm workers at the time. Despite this, there was no resentment of Blacke or of his remuneration.

Outside and beyond Henry's court, there were other examples of black people making their homes in England. Many of them owed their presence in England to the piratical and trading activities of English sailors on the African coast.

The first large group of Africans arrived in England in 1513. They came from the Iberian Peninsula, having originally been taken prisoner and removed from their homelands in West Africa, probably in chains, by Spanish and Portuguese merchants.

The Africans were employed mainly as servants and cattle herders and despite first appearing in the country as slaves, by the end of Henry's reign they had become integrated into English society.

There appears to have been no prejudice against these individuals, not in the manner that the 'strangers' had been targeted in London in 1517 or in the way that the small Jewish groups had been pilloried and then exiled at the end of Henry VIII's reign. By the middle years of the sixteenth century, they were accepted members of the local communities where they lived, particularly in London and seaports like Southampton and Bristol.

Being small in number – probably no more than three or four hundred in total – the 'blackamores' as they were known did not pose a threat to any individual or group. And that meant they had no direct involvement in any of the disturbances during the reign of Henry VIII.

Chapter Six

The Amicable Grant and the Beginning of an End

Henry VIII was nothing if not the supreme opportunist. All of his life he had taken chances, revelling in conquering the unknown and enjoying his unexpected victories. Only when things went wrong did he stop to analyse and, occasionally, regret his actions. But regret was a rare emotion, there were advisors and friends to blame when things went badly wrong.

One regret, however, stayed with him forever. He had never forgotten the humiliation of losing his wrestling match with the French king at the Field of Cloth of Gold and had always vowed that when the opportunity came to strike at Francis, he would seize it with both hands. That opportunity finally came in the winter of 1525.

In February the French had been defeated at the Battle of Pavia by Charles V of Spain, the newly crowned Holy Roman Emperor. Henry had put his name forward for election to the position of Holy Roman Emperor but had lost out to the wealthier and more influential Charles. He had been angry at the time, offended by what he regarded as a dismissive response to his application, but this defeat of the French provided him with some measure of compensation.

Losing the battle was one thing but it was made even worse for the French when Francis was captured by Emperor Charles's forces. Not for Henry:

When the messenger brought the news of Francis I's capture to Henry VIII the King is reported to have been likened to the Archangel Gabriel, such was his happiness and excitement at hearing the news.[1]

This was Henry's chance to gain his revenge, the Great Enterprise as it became known. He would declare war on France, humiliate Francis even more and possibly even claim back the French throne. There was just one flaw to his plan. Money – or, rather, lack of it!

Together, Henry and Wolsey discussed the situation, eventually deciding that what was needed was a sum close to £800,000 to enable the king to wage his war. Henry was happy with that figure and gave Wolsey 'the nod'. And at that point the king found himself hoisted on his own petard.

He had consciously given Parliament power such as it had never known before and now the Commons showed that they understood exactly how to exercise that power. They would not grant the king money.

Previous campaigns against France in 1522 and 1523 had been largely unsuccessful and the forced loans extracted at that time, somewhere in the region of £250,000 to £300,000 had not been repaid. Indeed, the subsidy for 1523 was still in the process of being collected. And now Wolsey and the king were looking for ways to raise more!

Wolsey's answer to the problem was to extend the subsidy concept which had been so successful and levy an extra tax on the people of Henry's dominion. This was over and above the annual subsidy which until that moment had been both effective and relatively painless.

Wolsey's new subsidy was to come in the form of what he saw as monetary gifts from the king's subjects in England and Wales. The gifts would be made to the monarch, without strings and obligations and certainly with no thoughts of recompense or repayment. It was to be given in order to allow Henry to take the country into yet another war.

The process became known as the Amicable Grant, a levy that would not be put to Parliament for its approval but which would be landed fairly and squarely on the shoulders of the king's subjects. It was a disguised tax, an amicable gift or a friendly and respectful offering – even though the people had absolutely no say in the matter.

The clergy would be expected to contribute one-third of their income, a quarter if that income was less than £10 a year. The well-off laity would pay 3s 4d in the pound if their land or business brought in over £50 annually, 2s 8d if their income was between £20 and £50. For anyone earning less than £20 a year the figure for their 'gift' to the crown was one shilling in the pound. That was the majority of the nation and in a time of economic hardship, it was a sum they could not easily find.

To Wolsey, it was a simple enough process, a logical and easy way of raising money, but he had reckoned without the strength of feeling in the populace. People quickly declared that yet another tax was a financial burden that was too great and, more importantly, was unconstitutional as the tax had been levied without the approval of Parliament.

The discontent had begun with the church when Archbishop Warham told Henry that the clergy of Kent were not inclined to pay the grant. It was, they believed, out of order as the matter had not been put to and approved by Convocation. Apart from that, the church had already been heavily taxed and this extra demand was, quite simply, one request too far.

The heads of religious houses such as monasteries, convents, abbeys and priories were also unhappy with the Amicable Grant, informing Warham that they would not contribute. Traditionally places where the poor could receive succour, it was not long before the discontent began to seep out from the walls of the monasteries and other religious houses.

As the trouble spread, so it increased in fervour. The inhabitants of Ely declared that, if they were obliged to do so, they *would* pay the Grant but that they would have to sell their cattle and farming equipment in order to meet the demand. And if they were forced to take that step it would cause poverty across the region. Inevitably, such action was bound to rebound and fall back on the government.

The discontent reached its most dangerous levels in the eastern counties of Essex, Kent, Norfolk, Warwickshire and Huntingdonshire. There Wolsey's Amicable Grant met, not with reluctance but with a downright refusal to pay. In Suffolk, peasants gathered together in truculent groups and muttered openly about rebellion. East Anglia was soon a seething mass of resentment with the possibility of rebellion against the crown a distinct likelihood.

The most serious riot or near-rebellion occurred in the market town of Lavenham in Suffolk. Almost 10,000 people from the town, from the nearby countryside and from the county in general, gathered together to protest the Grant. Rebellion was close at hand, the word whispered by everyone. The ringing of the bells in Lavenham Church was supposedly the signal to march – although no one was quite sure where they were going to march to!

According to legend a local nobleman called Sir John Spring managed to save the day by removing the clappers of the church bells so that they would not ring. Consequently, the would-be rebels gathered together but went nowhere! True or false, it makes a great story but the real saviours of the situation were the two major landowners from East Anglia, the Dukes of Suffolk and Norfolk.

The Duke of Suffolk was first on hand. While waiting for the more powerful Norfolk to arrive he set about preparing for war, destroying bridges, erecting barricades and deploying his limited forces at strategic points around Lavenham.

Suffolk may have given the impression of confidence and assurance but secretly he was worried. He wrote to Cardinal Wolsey expressing the opinion that he doubted if his soldiers – mostly just retainers and part-time warriors from the local area – would be prepared to fight against their fellow countrymen.

In the end, the Duke of Norfolk arrived with his more professional troops and after negotiations with the rebels and a few bouts of fisticuffs, the protesters were sent packing. Several of the leaders were arrested and immediately despatched to London where they were flung into Fleet Prison. The Grant was not collected.

The gathering of the Suffolk rioters at Lavenham was one of the few successful rebellions – if rebellion it was – to take place in England during the Tudor period. It did not remove the king, that was never its intention, but it did achieve its primary aim of stopping the application and collection of the Amicable Grant.

The rising had been led by artisans and peasants, an unusual event in Tudor England when most serious disturbances had nobles, gentry or professional people at their head. It was altogether a most rare event.

* * *

The Lavenham protesters might have been dispersed but the point had been made – there was only so much that the king's subjects were prepared to take. Clearly, Thomas Wolsey had misjudged the situation. He was not prepared to lose face, however, and despite what had happened at Lavenham he insisted that the Amicable Grant should continue to be collected.

In London the news was met with more discontent and mobs of angry men and women gathered menacingly at street corners where they chanted and hurled abuse at anyone who seemed to have official status. Henry was alarmed and immediately halved the tax demands. It did little to calm the situation and it was not long before the king was forced to abandon the collection of the Amicable Grant altogether.

The climb down was spectacular but there was more to come. It was time now for another theatrical show, not unlike the one that had ended the Evil May Day affair in 1517.

At the end of May 1525, the ringleaders from the Suffolk protests were brought before the *Court of Star Chamber*. Cardinal Wolsey led what became a ceremony of reconciliation, an ostentatious and spectacular affair where he begged the king to forgive and pardon his fellow Suffolk men. Henry, claiming that he had known nothing about the Grant, graciously agreed. Unlike the Evil May Day affair, such a decision may not have resulted in exultation and joy in the streets but most people nodded sagely and commended the king for his wisdom and judgement.

It was brilliantly played out, Wolsey wringing his hands and pleading for leniency, the king listening intently before finally nodding his head. What was not known was that Wolsey had actually supplied the main protesters with money to pay for their lodgings and food while they were in London and Henry had already decided on his response before the hearings even began.

Throughout it all Wolsey managed to put a brave face on things but it was a bitter blow for him. The failure of the Amicable Grant was the first time any of his schemes had ended badly, the first time he had been unable to enact the king's will.

Henry may have played the part of the gracious sovereign but inside he was seething. As a result of the debacle of the Amicable Grant, he was forced to abandon his long-cherished dream of humiliating King Francis and now he saw no alternative but to sign a peace treaty with France.

To rub salt in the wound the Treaty of More was signed for the French by Louise of Savoy, the temporary regent, as Francis was still being held in captivity. Henry could only lament his missed opportunity and pretend to be happy with the agreement. It was reluctantly done.

Henry knew that he had been lucky to avoid a serious rebellion. With the eastern provinces of the country up in arms against the Grant, it would not have taken much for the dissension to spread. All it would have needed was one quick victory for the protesters, at Lavenham or elsewhere, and Henry would have been fighting to retain his throne.

What really hurt, however, was the simple fact that the humiliation which Henry had intended for the King of France had rounded on him. The cause of that disaster was easy to identify, his trusty confidant Cardinal Wolsey. And Henry neither forgot nor forgave such a blow to his ego.

Henry did not suffer unduly as a result of his about-turn over the Amicable Grant or from his overly gracious and magnanimous climb down in front of *Star Chamber*. That was an act, a hugely effective act, but his subjects were not aware of the king's double-dealing – and for him, there was always the thought that one day he would exact revenge for his humiliation.

Meanwhile, just as he had done after the Evil May Day hearings Henry emerged from the crisis as the noble, understanding and fair-minded monarch that everyone wanted him to be. And, of course, he was doubly lucky – he had a ready-made scapegoat, someone who could and would take the blame for him.

If Wolsey had been unpopular with the people, commoners as well as nobles, before the debacle of the Amicable Grant, now he was almost universally reviled.

Increasingly, people saw him as a self-interested, bloated sycophant living in great style while they struggled through life, enduring the imposition of taxes like the Amicable Grant.

If proof of Wolsey's self-indulgence was needed people only had to look at his grand and luxurious house on the banks of the Thames a few miles outside London. Hampton Court was a palace fit for a king and, in keeping with its grandeur, Wolsey was later to present it as a gift to Henry. If the present was an attempt to retain the approval and favour of the king it did not work – and the people of England knew it.

Wolsey was to remain as Lord Chancellor for a further five years but there is no doubt that his position as Henry's chief advisor had been undermined by his failure to impose the Amicable Grant. The king never felt quite the same again about his chancellor and while he would continue to use him as long as he was useful, Wolsey's inability to come up with the money for his war with France was a failure that rankled with the king. Henry did not like failure and now, in hindsight, it is clear that this was the beginning of the end for the cardinal.

More than anything, even though Henry continued to defer to him in domestic matters, Wolsey's actions in the last few years of his life did little more than antagonise the nobility of the land. He would cause them significant discontent and anger, adding more and more names to the list of those who counted themselves as his enemy.

None of them had liked or approved of Thomas Wolsey, even before he began to falter in the king's eyes. He was a common man, someone from the lower ranks of society and yet despite this he had more control and influence than all of them put together. Until, that is, the failure of the Amicable Grant opened up his underbelly and made him suddenly vulnerable.

That was when the whispering began. All his life Henry had been susceptible to the 'whisper in the ear' and now the great nobles, Norfolk, Suffolk and the rest, began to ply him with negative comments and information about Wolsey. Henry listened and made mental notes but for the moment did nothing. He still needed the wily cardinal.

Wolsey ploughed steadily onwards, continuing to upset and annoy the nobles, seemingly at every turn. In reality, he was fighting for his life, knowing the likely fate of those who had failed the king or were no longer useful to him.

He was already suspicious of what he regarded as 'the myrmidons', the young newcomers to court and to the Privy Council, feeling – accurately enough – that they were out to undermine his position. He was isolated and alone, unable to trust anyone. Not even the smooth and oily words of his assistant and arch manipulator Thomas Cromwell could ease the concerns.

In the Eltham Ordinances of 1526, Wolsey struck out at the nobility and cut the number of Privy Councillors from twelve to just six. The nobles responded with fury and anger but they could do nothing in practical terms. Wolsey still had the king's ear, even more so now when access to that ear had been limited, and as long as that was the case, they were helpless to make an efficient and effective protest.

Wolsey annoyed the great nobles even further by opposing the increasing desire to convert their lands from arable to pastoral farming. Landowners had rented out their land to tenant farmers for hundreds of years in a time-honoured process, one of the last remnants of feudalism, a tradition that was part of a clearly defined social system. Now, however, the nobles wanted to enclose as much territory as possible and turn their land into pastures and grazing land for sheep.

Enclosures had been a potential landmine for years but the dire economic situation in the 1520s and 30s brought the issue to a new level and created enormous tensions in rural society. Enclosures became a smoking gun that was regularly cocked and equally as regularly went off.

At the beginning of the sixteenth century, prices were high, profits were low and the landowners were receiving poor returns on their investments. The idea of enclosing land previously used by the peasants for arable farming seemed like an easy way out of the dilemma. The future, great landowners had decided, lay in sheep.

Wolsey's objection to enclosures and the sudden increase of pastoral farming earned him more hatred from the great landowners and noblemen. He had already forced through anti-enclosure legislation in 1515 and 1517 and now, in the wake of the Amicable Grant, did so again in 1526.

All in all, Wolsey oversaw the passing of five such pieces of legislation designed to limit the number and style of enclosures. The fact that it required so many different passages of law was proof that the nobles either ignored or else deliberately flouted the new legislation. Whatever their motivation or intention it remains clear that the gap between Wolsey and the great and good of the nation widened considerably in these final years of his life.

The peasants and tenant farmers did not take the changes lying down. There was an increased number of anti-enclosure riots during the late 1520s but they did little to help Wolsey's position.

The peasants and small farmers failed to see him as their champion and took out their frustration in direct action. It seemed at times as if there was a continual feeling of discontent and disorder in the country, even though the riots were not aimed at the King or his government:

Enclosure riots, at least prior to the riots and rebellion of 1548-49, were not particularly directed against the governing elite, but rather were aimed at innovations which threatened the traditional agrarian routine within the manorial or village economy … (they) did not especially menace the social order.[2]

Perhaps it would have been better for Wolsey if the riots had been more significant. The moment the king and his court were perceived to be under threat he could, then, have sent in the troops and cut out the problem at its source.

As it was, the issue of enclosures remained a niggling thorn in his side right to the end. The anti-enclosure riots were put down easily enough, the vast majority resolved at local level. And when, in 1549, matters did finally come to a violent conclusion in the shape of Kett's Rebellion both Wolsey and Henry were already dead.

Viewed now in hindsight it seems as if Wolsey was being stymied at every turn. Reforms in the justice system did not help his situation, either. By following the king's directives and making justice available to all, Wolsey simply overloaded the system with all the paraphernalia of minor, time-consuming complaints.

Eventually, in 1538 he responded to the problem by ordering the removal of all minor cases from the Court of Star Chamber. They could be better dealt with at local magistrate's courts, he judged, where the less significant nobles would happily assume the roles of Justices of the Peace.

It was a sensible enough move but the great nobles immediately took it personally. They felt that their rights, as the effective controllers of the most significant court in the land, were once again being challenged and destroyed by Thomas Wolsey. The result? More fury, more whisperings and a step closer to the final downfall.

When you add in the problems created by the Boleyn family and the question of Henry's marriage to Catherine of Aragon – more of this later – by the final years of the 1520s Wolsey must have felt that the whole world was against him. He was floundering in deep water and he knew it.

Chapter Seven

Wicked Witchcraft and a Little Heresy

B y the time Henry VIII became king the fear of witchcraft had been common for years. The Bible had laid the ground, Genesis 22:18 making the injunction 'Thou shalt not suffer a witch to live' By the close of the fifteenth century, the Spanish Inquisition had created an atmosphere across the length and breadth of Europe where those biblical lines were taken quite literally. Find a witch, kill a witch, that was the general tenor or attitude of the age.

A 1484 proclamation by Pope Innocent VIII moved things up a gear, the Papacy denouncing witches and calling for vigorous measures to be taken against them. Two members of the Inquisition instantly produced what became *the* handbook about witchcraft and the way it should be dealt with. *Malleus Maleficarum* was soon being regarded as the witch-finders 'Bible'.

The Reformation is commonly regarded as starting in 1517 when Martin Luther nailed his Ninety-Five Theses to the door of the Castle Church in Wittenberg. Protestantism was born, concentrating on Justification by Faith rather than by works and deeds. Amongst other things it led to both sides of the religious schism, Protestants and Catholics alike, accusing each other of fostering witchcraft. *Malleus Maleficarum* showed potential witch-hunters how to hunt out and destroy witches. It also showed how to score important points off the 'other side'.

There were relatively few instances of witchcraft in England during the reign of Henry VIII and although the *Malleus Maleficarum* was available to church dignitaries and to officers of the Crown it seems to have been rarely used. When accusations of witchcraft did occur perhaps the most infamous and damaging of them were related to the top elements of society. To the end of her life, the stigma of necromancy and witchcraft surrounded no less a figure than Queen Anne Boleyn.

Such allegations against women of significance and power were not exactly an unusual occurrence. Hints and allegations had been common enough for years but they were not, generally, related to the eternal conflict between superstition and cold hard reasoning. There was a far more prosaic rationale at work.

In 1419 the unpopular Joanna or Joan of Navarre, wife of Henry IV had been arrested on suspicion of witchcraft. Due to the death of the king, she was never tried for the necromancy of which she was accused but even so her stepson, Henry V, kept her locked away in prison. Only on his deathbed did he finally relent and order her release. Joanna was not the only victim.

Eleanor Cobham, wife of the Duke of Gloucester, was accused of using potions to make the duke fall in love with her while Elizabeth Woodville, the first commoner to become Queen Consort of England, also carried with her the taint of witchcraft. Why else would the handsome and powerful Edward IV fall so deeply in love with a woman with so few connections?

The casting of spells, necromancy and witchcraft might seem to be almost an occupational hazard in this superstitious age but there was a distinctly political edge to the accusations:

Allegations of witchcraft (were used) as a means of curtailing the power of prominent women throughout the fifteenth century.[1]

Bearing that in mind it was perhaps inevitable that Anne Boleyn should fall foul of the rumour machine. Unlike her predecessor Catherine of Aragon, Anne was never a popular figure.

To a large number of people in the country, Anne's machinations and desire to be queen had ended the king's marriage and, ultimately, England's links with the Catholic church. It was, therefore, no surprise when rumours and stories about the supernatural dabbling of the would-be queen began to circulate.

The Boleyn family were members of the minor nobility but Thomas Boleyn, father of Anne, was hugely ambitious and quickly became active in Henry's court where he was renowned as a diplomat and courier. Initially, the king took Mary, the eldest of Thomas's two daughters, as a mistress but as doubts about the inability of his wife to provide him with an heir began to grow, it was towards Anne Boleyn that his amorous glances were increasingly cast. Henry's seven-year-long pursuit of her began in earnest in March 1526.

The story of Henry's break with Rome is well known. When Wolsey failed to provide Henry with an annulment – not, as is usually thought, a divorce – the king went his own way and declared himself Supreme Head of the Church in England. He could then announce, and genuinely believe, that his marriage to Catherine was null and void on grounds that the Bible had made clear to everyone.

On pain of his immortal soul, declared the Bible, no man should ever marry his brother's wife. Therefore, the scriptures showed that the previous Pope, Julius II, had not had the right or the power to offer the dispensation which had permitted the marriage of Henry and Catherine.

One of the great tragedies of Henry's reign was that he remained, until the end of his life, a hugely devout Catholic. He retained his belief, convinced that he had incurred God's displeasure by marrying Catherine of Aragon.

Above all Henry was pragmatic and knew that Catherine could not provide him with the male heir he desired, the heir who would protect the country from a return to the Wars of the Roses. Marriage and fathering a son with Anne Boleyn were the only way forward. The fact that he was, on both a physical and emotional level, obsessed with her was largely irrelevant.

In an intensely religious and spiritual age, the break with Rome was a terrible blow to the people of England and Wales. It was cutting away the traditional and known structures of their lives, customs that had made them feel safe and content – even if they could not understand the language of the service or the deeper aspects of the faith. They could hardly vent their anger and displeasure on the king; Anne Boleyn was a different matter.

Anne was crowned queen on 1 June 1533. The previous day she had taken part in an elaborate and magnificent procession through London, sitting in state in a litter lined with white cloth of gold. To say that the response of the public was lukewarm is an understatement. Anne and Henry pretended not to notice the silence that greeted the soon-to-be queen as she passed through the city but by then it was too late. The mutterings and defamatory comments had already begun.

As the years progressed and Anne failed to give Henry more than one daughter, the king's disquiet grew along with the rumours. Anne had bewitched the king, people claimed, in order to get him to marry her and it seemed as if Henry agreed. The French ambassador, Eustace Chapuys, recorded Henry's own feelings on the matter:

> He had made this marriage, he said, seduced and constrained by sortilege (spells) and for this reason he held the said marriage void … This accursed lady has so enchanted and bewitched him that he will not dare to do anything against her will.[2]

Seduced and sortilege, enchanted and bewitched – those were powerful words but Henry was speaking after Anne's second or third miscarriage when he was still emotionally distraught. And, of course, Chapuys was giving Francis his master exactly what the French king wanted to hear. His report, therefore, must be considered a little suspect.

The views of Henry's subjects soon moved from dislike to emotions bordering on hatred, particularly when Anne failed to provide a male heir – which was, in their eyes, the sole purpose of her existence. Soon they were calling her 'the King's whore' and other less savoury names.

Anne sailed blithely on, living and holding court in great style at the Palace of Placentia in Greenwich where she was waited on by over 250 servants and maids-in-waiting. In total contrast, the now rejected Catherine passed her days in quiet dignity and isolation. To Henry's subjects, Anne's behaviour simply reinforced their opinion of her as a 'gold digger' and harlot.

Stories continued to circulate. Anne's third miscarried child, it was said, had been just a shapeless mass of flesh, the product not of a human act of love but the still-born child of the Devil. When news of the death of Catherine of Aragon reached her at the Palace of Placentia, it was reported – and almost universally accepted – that Anne was unable to control her joy:

> Queen Anne rejoiced at the death of Catherine, the consort of her royal husband, because there could be no further dispute concerning that marriage.[3]

Such feelings may have been understandable as far as Anne was concerned but the king's subjects, who heard the story soon enough, were quick to attribute such unnatural emotions to someone in league with Satan. The late-Tudor writer Nicholas Sander added his own few pennyworths to the legends with a more than defamatory picture of Queen Anne:

> She was rather tall of stature with black hair and an oval face of sallow complexion, as if troubled with jaundice. She had a projecting tooth under her upper lip, and on her right hand six fingers. There was a large wen (wart) under her chin and therefore to hide its ugliness she wore a high dress covering her throat.[4]

Sander, a committed Catholic, had a vested interest in painting Anne in as black a light as possible. Nevertheless, all the hallmarks of witchery are there in his words – the projecting tooth, the wart, the extra finger – and people believed him implicitly.

The portrait Sander paints of Anne Boleyn is little more than a caricature, an evil one at that. Most of it came from stories passed around by the public and eagerly picked up by this early chronicler. The rest of the picture came from his own fertile imagination.

It is highly unlikely that Henry would ever have fallen in love with such a creature as that described by Nicholas Sander, a cliched picture of a witch if ever there was one. Sander's words need to be taken with a considerable measure of salt!

In 1536 when Anne Boleyn was imprisoned and executed by the king, he had already fallen in love again, this time with Jane Seymour. Always susceptible to flattery and a pretty face, Henry undoubtedly fell in love as often as he pulled on new shoes but he needed to find a rationale for his change in affections. 'Bad mouthing' the woman who until recently had been the love of his life was only to be expected.

The English people did not exactly celebrate Anne's passing but the rancour and dislike remained. The witch is dead, seemed to be the general consensus, praise the Lord, the witch is dead. Very few remembered her with affection and the taint of witchcraft was far stronger than any real-life memories that might have survived.

When Anne fell from favour, her life ended at the hands of a French swordsman, she stood accused of adultery, incest and treason. The charge of witchcraft was never formally made against her but it was there, in the background, hovering like a spell and has never yet gone away.

* * *

The first Witchcraft Act in England was passed in 1542, four years before the death of Henry VIII. It was the first Act of Parliament to define witchcraft as a felony rather than a religious offence and to make it a crime punishable by death.

The success or failure of previous prosecutions had always depended on the aim and seriousness of the particular piece of alleged sorcery. Being a witch had not been a particular problem. How the witch powers were used certainly was.

Dealing with witchcraft had always been something of a minefield for the church and for would-be witch-hunters. Using sorcery to bring about the illness or death of another person was common enough. Bewitching someone into an action they would otherwise never have taken or causing farm animals to suddenly sicken and die might be less serious but both were even more common.

All three instances of spells and witchcraft might well have their origins in the machinations of someone in league with the Devil but they might equally result in different styles and levels of punishment. It depended on intent, on the views of a particular judge and on things like the mood of the country at a particular moment. Now, as a result of the new Act, simply being a witch could be enough to warrant the death penalty.

The Act was quite specific in its definitions and in the activities that would not be tolerated. People were forbidden to engage in any of the following:

> To use, devyse, practise or exercise, or cause to be devysed, practised or exercised any invovacons or cojuracons of Sprites, witchcrafts, enchauntementes or sorcises to the intent to fynde money or treasure or to waste, consume or destroy any persone in his bodie members.[5]

If found guilty of being a witch, the punishment *could* be death. Capital punishment was an option but it was not a necessity.

Even after the death of Henry, in the years when witch-hunting became commonplace, there were not really that many witch-related executions. Between 1560 and 1700 only 112 witches were actually executed out of a total of 513 that were brought to court. The death of even one unfortunate woman was one death too many but state persecution of witches in England was not really the stuff of which witch hunts were made.

During the reign of Henry VIII capital punishment for witchcraft meant death by hanging, not as is usually believed burning at the stake, although the burning of witches was permitted in Scotland. Torture was also prohibited in witchcraft cases but again both torture and burning were considered acceptable in cases of heresy and treason – and, unfortunately for the accused, there the lines between the various offences blurred somewhat.

Elizabeth Barton, the so-called *Nun of Kent* or *The Holy Maid of Kent*, was one woman who straddled the delicate line between heresy and witchcraft. She eventually suffered the fate of hanging, the witch's punishment, but only after considerable amounts of torture.

Born near Canterbury in 1506, Elizabeth began having visions in 1525 when she was just nineteen years old. She had been working as a maidservant for a farmer by the name of Thomas Cobb when she became seriously ill, falling into and out of comas or drugged sleep. In her delirious fevers, she claimed to have been given divine revelations. These ranged from prophesying the death of a child in Cobb's house to heartfelt pleas for people to remain loyal to the Catholic Church.

Recovered from her sickness Elizabeth spoke about the sanctity and power of the Mass and urged people, for the sake of their souls, to undertake pilgrimages. With the Reformation in Germany and the Low Countries making huge inroads into the power of Catholicism and with Henry already clear about his desire to distance himself from Catherine these were potentially dangerous words for any lay person to utter – and a lay woman, at that.

It had not been many years since Joan of Arc had been burned at the stake for claiming to hear voices and the link between religious fervour and witchcraft was too close for comfort. It was decidedly dangerous ground. Nevertheless, thousands believed in the *Holy Maid of Kent* and came to Canterbury just to listen to her words.

Both William Warham, the Archbishop of Canterbury, and John Fisher, Bishop of Rochester, attested to the fact that Elizabeth Barton had led and continued to lead a pious life. Warham even went as far as to appoint a commission to ascertain that Elizabeth's prophesies were not at variance with the teachings of the Catholic Church. The result was favourable for Elizabeth and Archbishop Warham duly arranged for her to be received into the Benedictine Priory at Canterbury.

Vagabonds and beggars in Tudor England.

Catherine of Aragon, beloved by the subjects of Henry, not so much by the man himself.

Thomas Cromwell, evil genius or honest servant of the crown – take your pick.

Thomas Seymour, Earl of Buckingham.

Elizabeth Barton, the Maid of Kent, a somewhat erotic print from the time.

Jane Seymour, third wife of Henry VIII.

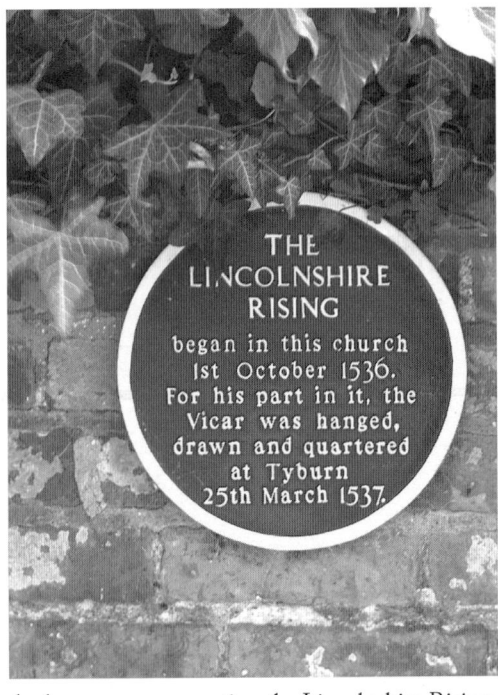

A plaque commemorating the Lincolnshire Rising.

Sir Thomas More, man for all seasons.

The Battle of Flodden Field where the Scots were defeated, James IV of Scotland killed and Thomas Howard regained his land and title of Duke of Norfolk.

One of the banners made for the pilgrims during the Pilgrimage of Grace.

The order and maner of the burning of Anne Askew, Iohn Lacels, Iohn Adams, Nicholas Belenian, with certayne of the Councell sitting in Smithfield.

Anne Askew is put to the flames.

Anne Boleyn, second wife of Henry.

Prince Arthur, eldest son of Henry VIII.

A contemporary painting depicting the Field of Cloth of Gold.

Beggars being whipped out of town, a common sight in Tudor England.

Cardinal Thomas Wolsey in all his pomp.

Edward VI, son of Henry VIII, the unwitting, unknowing cause of so much hardship.

The most awful of all Tudor punishments, being boiled alive!

The deadly duo, Empson and Dudley with Henry VII, their master.

Evil May Day, the riots in London begin.

Henry's great rival, Francis I of France.

The remains of Glastonbury Abbey, one of hundreds of similar establishments destroyed in the Dissolution of the Monasteries.

Erasmus, the great scholar and friend/tutor to Henry VIII.

Thomas Howard, Duke of Norfolk, soldier of the King.

Henry VIII – as he wanted to be seen.

The young, fit and active Henry VIII.

i444.—Henry and Anne sending Dr. Butts with token of favour to the sick Cardnial.

Henry, Anne Boleyn and Dr Butts, friend and advisor to the King.

Henry in old age, fat, out of condition and destined not to live much longer.

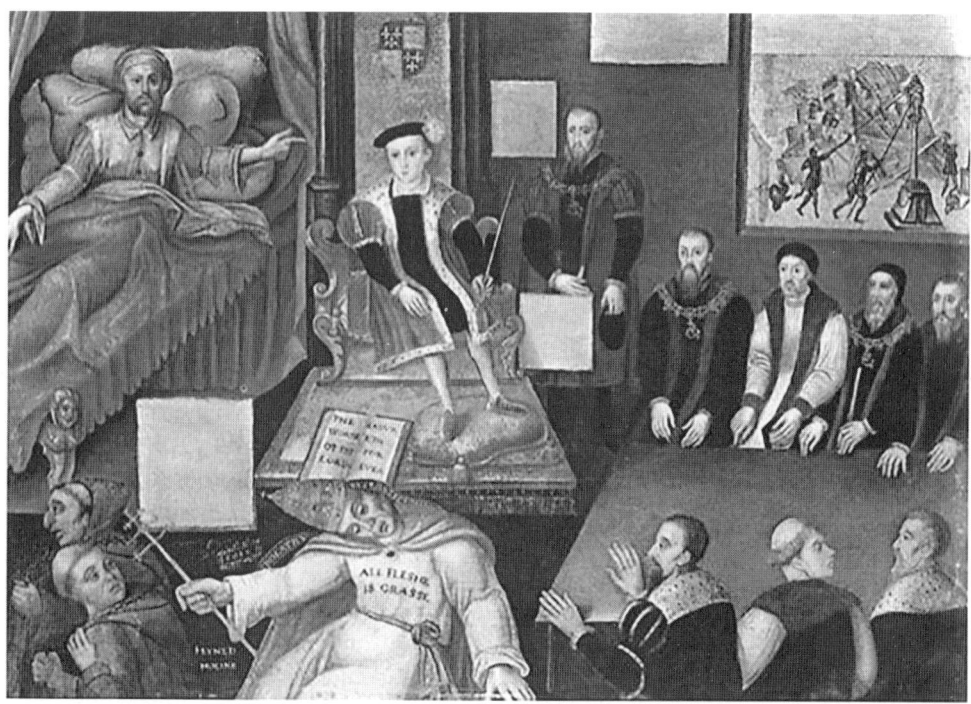

The death of Henry VIII.

The bloody and botched execution of Margaret Pole, a contemporary print.

Rioting – a perpetual problem in Tudor England.

A contemporary print showing the Pilgrimage of Grace.

Monastery closed; the ransacking can begin!

Henry feared rebellion and strove to keep it at bay – not always successfully as this print shows.

Medieval society – the Reeve and the peasants.

Rhys ap Gruffydd, Welsh rebel and opponent of the King.

Bishop John Fisher, one of the great clergymen of Henry's reign.

Sheep – the innocent cause of so much trouble.

Archbishop Thomas Cranmer, one of the architects of the English Reformation, destined to die in the flames of Mary's retaliation.

Thomas Fitzgerald, the Silken Earl.

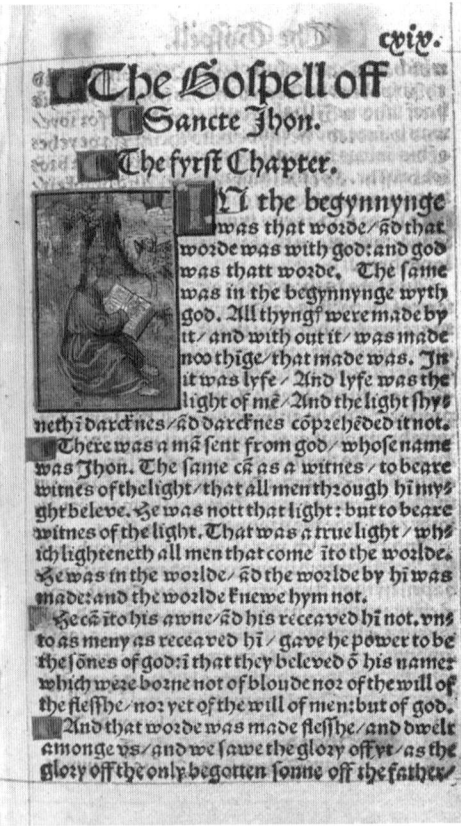

A page from the Tyndale Bible.

Matters escalated when Henry's desire to achieve an annulment to his marriage became common knowledge. At the centre of the issue, as everyone knew, was Anne Boleyn. Kings had always taken mistresses without undue concern or comment but for some reason, Anne Boleyn aroused the fury of Henry's subjects almost from the beginning.

When Anne became linked with what everyone considered the king's 'divorce' – *the King's Great Matter* as it was known – the fury increased. Like so many hundreds of the king's subjects across the country Elizabeth Barton was violently opposed to the rise of Anne Boleyn and in the summer of 1532, she began to prophesy that if Henry was to abandon Catherine and marry her, he would die within a few months. That was a potentially fatal combination of heresy, treason and witchcraft.

Such was Elizabeth's fame that a book was produced about her prophesies. Written by Father Edward Bocking, later executed along with her, only 700 copies were ever printed and these were seized by Cromwell and destroyed. No copies now remain in existence.

On several occasions, Elizabeth Barton was called to meet with King Henry and with both Thomas Wolsey and Sir Thomas More. The latter, when later accused of consorting with the Maid, was adamant that they had spoken only about theological matters and that he had told her in no uncertain terms to stay well clear of the king's business.

Despite More's warning, Elizabeth's opposition to England breaking away from the Catholic Church and the authority of the Pope was obvious to everyone. She would not keep such beliefs to herself and it was not something that Henry would tolerate for long.

Agents of the king began to spread rumours that Elizabeth had often engaged in sexual relationships with priests and that she was renowned as being mentally unbalanced. Finally, in 1533 she was arrested and taken to the Tower.

There Elizabeth Barton was tortured, the actions being overseen – although not inflicted – by Thomas Cromwell. Under the terrible pain of torture, she finally admitted to making false prophesies but then claimed that God had revealed to her that he no longer recognised Henry as King of England.

One of the witnesses brought against her was Friar John Lawrence. His evidence was damning but he then rather spoiled that evidence by requesting to be given one of the posts left vacant by the arrest of Barton's fellow observants!

Elizabeth, the *Holy Maid of Kent*, was condemned under a Bill of Attainder, an Act of Parliament authorising punishment without trial. She was hanged at Tyburn on 20 April 1534. She was twenty-eight years old. Five supporters were hanged along with her.

Before her execution, Elizabeth was taken to several of the major towns of England, beginning at St Paul's Cross in London, where she publicly repeated her confession before 2,000 witnesses, admitting to making false promises and prophesies. Inevitably, in the face of such a statement, her support fell away. Henry, who was concerned about a possible rising in her name, was satisfied.

Interestingly, the punishment administered to the *Holy Maid of Kent* was hanging. This was normally the punishment reserved for witches; heretics were burned at the stake. So where did that put Elizabeth Barton? The jury remains out but, after her death, Elizabeth's severed head was taken and displayed on London Bridge. She was the only woman ever to suffer such a fate.

*   *   *

Anne Askew was one of the last victims of Henry's paranoia, being martyred at the stake on 16 July 1546. A poet, writer and devout Protestant, as a young woman Anne had been married off to a man equally as devout – but, unfortunately for her, a confirmed Catholic. The marriage was doomed to fail and Anne eventually left the family home for London. In the city, she met other Protestants, including the Anabaptist John Bocker.

Under their influence, Anne Askew became a 'gospeler', preaching in the open air to anyone who would listen. She was arrested on a number of occasions and returned to her husband's home in Lincolnshire but always managed to escape again.

Finally, early in 1546, she was brought to the Tower. It was a time when Henry was planning an alliance with Charles V of Spain and did not want to annoy the Catholic subjects of the Spanish king and Holy Roman Emperor. It was also a time of reaction against the Protestant faith and Henry, near to death, was clearly regretting the break with Rome and all that it entailed. His Reformation was really nothing of the sort; all that had happened was the changing of the Pope for the English king.

As a possible Anabaptist, Anne Askew's views were far too dramatic and 'Protestant' for the king. Anabaptists were particularly feared because they claimed that the authority of the Holy Spirit lay within them. When asked if she, like John Bocker and others, acted with the Holy Spirit inside her, Anne's answer was both simple and chilling – 'If I did not, I was but a reprobate or cast awaye'.[6]

Even Henry's sixth and last wife, Catherine Parr, came under suspicion of being an active Protestant. The pro-Catholic faction at court was determined to snuff out all traces of Protestantism and in 1545 there was even a warrant drawn up for the queen's arrest. She had written a book, *Psalms or Prayers*, published anonymously, outlining the basics of her faith and for a while, there was a schism between her and the king. It was resolved and Catherine was reprieved.

Not so Anne Askew. After being interrogated several times, she was taken to the lower room of the White Tower where she was shown the dreaded rack. It was an attempt to intimidate her but when she refused to 'name names' or to admit that she was wrong in denying the sacrament, she was placed on the torture device.

When the torture began, Anne was pulled along the bed and lifted six inches into the air above the rack. She fainted from the pain and Sir Anthony Knevet, Lieutenant of the Tower, refused to continue. He immediately went to the king in an attempt to stop the brutality which was being inflicted on Anne Askew in his name.

Knevet's appeal did not stop the torture which was carried on by the Lord Chancellor Sir Thomas Wriothesley and by Sir Richard Rich, a man who had already betrayed Sir Thomas More and was later to become Chancellor himself.

The punishment inflicted on Anne Askew was indeed dreadful. Most of her joints were dislocated, her arms pulled from their sockets – and still, the torture continued.

Wriothesley and Rich were dearly hoping that she would implicate Queen Catherine Parr but even at the most agonising moments of her ordeal Anne named no one. Neither did she renounce any of her beliefs. Her intransigence was matched only by her courage.

In a final effort to break her spirit Anne Askew was removed to Newgate Prison:

> Anne arrived at a prison already centuries old and creaking with years of deterioration and neglect … Newgate was a harrowing place. It was crammed with souls, a perilous hive of disease in which criminals, debtors and religious prisoners like Anne were stuffed into fetid corridors and filthy cells.[7]

If her interrogators thought this would break her, they were gravely mistaken. More interrogation went on over several days and even when she went down with sickness caught in the prison Anne would say nothing, either to save herself or condemn others.

Finally, realising they were getting nowhere, the torturers ended Anne Askew's ordeal. She was convicted of heresy and condemned to be burned at the stake.

Anne Askew was executed, along with three other martyrs, at Smithfield on 16 July 1546. She had to be carried to the stake as she was unable to walk and then strapped into a chair in the middle of the fire. She maintained her dignity to the end.

Only as the flames finally reached her chest did Anne cry out in pain – and then the small bags of gunpowder concealed about her person exploded and ended her suffering.

The tragedy of Anne Askew's life and death was simply that she was too pious. She died for holding firmly to Protestant views in a country where the Pope had been dismissed but the dominant religion – and view of the king – remained Catholic.

*   *   *

The whole issue of 'holy women' and their effect on the populace remained significant throughout Henry's reign. Some were genuine in their beliefs, sure that they had received divine intervention. Others, like the so-called *Maid of Leominster* were clearly frauds. Either way, they created a frisson of tension and excitement that added another dimension to the disorder and fragile peace of early sixteenth-century England.

Early in the century, the Prior of Leominster installed the Maid, first name Elizabeth, last name unknown, in the rood loft of the Priory in Leominster. He claimed that the mysterious woman had been sent by God. She could, he said, survive without food or drink, living only on Angels Food or communion bread. At first glance, the claim seemed genuine enough.

The Maid did not descend to the chapel, either to eat or to pray, but during Mass bread was seen to fly up out of the Prior's hand into the Maid's mouth as she waited in the rood loft. Before anyone realised it a cult following had established itself around the fasting Maid. Thousands flocked to see her, coming from all over the country to seek cures for ailments and for blessings.

Such was the furore created by *the Maid of Leominster* that in 1517 the king's grandmother Lady Margaret Beaufort was commissioned by the Crown to form a council to investigate the bizarre phenomenon. Central government was concerned that, for the public, the miracle of the Maid was rapidly descending into a case of mass hysteria.

Under Lady Margaret's guidance and leadership, Sir John Neville, the Third Baron Latimer, quickly found that the case of the sainted, non-eating *Maid of Leominster* was certainly not a religious miracle. The Maid was nothing but a fraud.

Beneath her bed in the Priory, Sir John found bones and portions of meat but, more significantly, he also discovered a thin wire stretching up from the altar into the rood loft. When communion bread was attached to the wire it would seem to be flying through the air and when Elizabeth carefully positioned herself the offering went straight into her mouth. It was a clever and well-worked trick that had fooled thousands.

Faced with the evidence the Prior admitted that he and Elizabeth were lovers and that they had devised the whole plot. The pair were ordered to suffer public penance, walking through the streets of the town clad only in a white sheet and each holding a candle. Sir Thomas More was more punitive in his view. He believed the pair should have been burned at the stake.

Sometimes so-called 'holy women' were guilty of nothing more than mistaken fervour. These were, perhaps, the most difficult to investigate and to approve or condemn.

In the late 1520s a woman known now only as Helen, living in Tottenham outside the city of London, began to suffer trances and what she described as revelations. Frightened by these, Helen looked for help from Elizabeth Barton, *the Holy Maid of Kent*:

> Barton listened as her visitor spoke to her of what she had seen, before dismissing the events. "They were no revelations but plain illusions of the Devil" and Helen should "Cast them out of her mind."[8]

Helen went home and disappeared from the pages of history. *The Maid of Kent* went on to her own inevitable meeting with the king's executioner.

Joan Bocher was a friend of Elizabeth Barton who had fallen foul of the authorities on several occasions, mainly for distributing copies of Tyndale's banned translation of the New Testament.

Despite the ban, many Tyndale Bibles had been smuggled into England, usually in bundles of cloth, and circulated amongst Protestant circles. Merely to hold and handle one was a treasonable offence! However, to see and read the Bible in English, Joan believed, was the birthright of every native-born English man and woman.

Imprisoned and interrogated, she was eventually forced to take up residence in the house of Sir Richard Rich where he could investigate further. Neither he nor anyone else could find ways of making Joan change her radical, Anabaptist views. Even the new Archbishop of Canterbury, Thomas Cranmer, failed to affect her.

Despite living a highly dangerous and exposed life, Joan managed to survive the reign of Henry. Her luck finally ran out, however, in May 1556 when she was burned at the stake in Smithfield, a genuine radical evangelist whose fate when compared to the fraudulent *Maid of Leominster* seems to be totally out of proportion.

The reaction of the authorities was in direct relation to the potential threat of the 'holy women' and their supposedly divine revelations. Where these were of major proportions, as with the *Maid of Leominster*, the Crown moved quickly.

It remains difficult to see quite what disruption and disorder most of the religious zealots brought to Henry's realm. When all was said and done Joan Bocher was a mere Bible seller who, given enough rope, would eventually condemn herself.

And yet it takes a great deal for the voices of the poor to be listened to, not just in the Tudor age but in any period: 'They are too rough, too uncomfortable, too raw'.[9] And that was part of the problem with the Maid of Kent, Joan Bocher and the others.

Ultimately, the main purpose of strong central government was to maintain peace and prosperity within the country. Separating annoyance from threat was the main problem and, in a world where fact and fiction, superstition and reason, were often difficult to assess it was inevitable that mistakes would be made and that the innocent would sometimes suffer, perhaps even perish, along with the guilty.

Chapter Eight

Wild Wales and Ireland's Silken Thomas

Henry VIII was part Welsh, the Tudor dynasty having its roots on the Isle of Anglesey, Ynys Mon as it was known, off the North Wales coast. His own father had been born in Pembroke Castle and when he had launched his invasion in 1485, knowing where his best and most obvious support lay, it was to this part of the country that the first Tudor monarch came.

Henry VIII had, however, little affection for Wales and rarely visited this western edge of his dominion. In this, he was no different from any of the other Tudor monarchs but it was inevitable, when faced with such lack of interest, that sooner or later there would be some sort of reaction from the king's Welsh subjects.

Following the Battle of Bosworth Field in 1485, Henry VII had been content to leave the governing of Wales to his compatriot and fellow Bosworth veteran, Sir Rhys ap Thomas. He might have been born in the Principality but by forcing his way to the Crown of England Henry Tudor had effectively abandoned his homeland for greater spoils and treasures. That more than suited Rhys ap Thomas who was content to govern the country in the name of his great friend.

For many years it was claimed that Sir Rhys was the man who had delivered the death stroke to Richard III. It was part of the romance of Henry's fight for the crown but while the King always called Rhys 'father', and often referred to him as being at the centre of the action throughout the battle, that claim now seems unlikely.

Rhys had been knighted by Henry once victory was assured and, after Bosworth, he went on to hold a number of offices in Wales. The most notable of these was Governor of All Wales but he was also one of the king's Privy Councillors. From his two main bases at Carew Castle in Pembrokeshire and Dinefwr in Carmarthenshire Sir Rhys, a Welshman and a man of the people, did a fine job for the monarchy in controlling and keeping the country peaceful.

His influence was not restricted to Wales. He took part in the military campaigns against Lambert Simnel and Perkin Warbeck and went on to fight with Henry VIII during his 1513 war in France. He was present at the Field of Cloth of Gold but a few years later died peacefully in his bed. That was when the troubles began.

Sir Rhys's son, Gruffydd ap Rhys ap Thomas had died in 1521, meaning that the sole remaining male in the family line was Rhys ap Gruffydd. Young, cocky, self-opinionated, he confidently expected to step into his grandfather's shoes. He was angry and devastated, therefore, when Henry VIII confounded expectation and passed on most of the estates, titles and offices in Wales to Walter Devereux, Lord Ferrers.

The reasons for Henry's decision are not clear. In all probability, he had been alerted by Wolsey or some other acolyte to a certain 'slackness' in Rhys' personality and did not feel happy entrusting him with control of his western seaboard. If that was indeed the case, Henry had not reckoned on the delayed adolescent pride of Rhys ap Gruffydd.

What began as bad feeling and jealousy between Rhys and Walter Devereux soon escalated into a full-scale feud where the disgruntled Rhys attempted to claw back some of his lost prestige and status. He petitioned Cardinal Wolsey to be given various posts but all that happened was that he was granted the right to increase the number of retainers in his household.

To someone like Rhys ap Gruffydd, married to Catherine, the daughter of the powerful and warlike Thomas Howard, Duke of Norfolk, that was a miniscule offering, a mere sop to his wounded pride. Catherine, well-schooled in the ways of medieval politics, undoubtedly fuelled her husband's feelings of disgruntlement. It did not take much. Arrogant and full of anger, Rhys saw Wolsey's actions as a further blow to his status and position in Wales.

To make matters worse, Walter Devereux or Lord Ferrers as he became, was given the same right. He, too, could now extend his personal army. Far from placating the 'cold shouldered' Rhys, all that the cardinal's gift had achieved was to create two competing armed gangs in a potentially lethal environment far away from the strictures and controls of London.

Matters reached crisis point in the summer of 1529 as, with his usual love of pomp and style, Walter Devereux began to prepare for the annual Court of Great Sessions in the West Wales market town of Carmarthen.

Rhys ap Gruffydd had been fuming and simmering for some time but this ostentatious show of power and status by his rival was the final straw.

Devereux might not have done it deliberately but with every trumpet blast and every parading of the Ferrers colours through Carmarthen town the message was driven home to Rhys ap Gruffydd – Walter Devereux was in control. Every swaggering man-at-arms in the livery of the Ferrers family who passed him in the street simply reinforced in Rhys the impression that Devereux was revelling in the prestige and the glamour that should have been his.

At last, unable to contain his anger any longer, Rhys and forty of his armed retainers confronted and surrounded Walter Devereux. Pulling out his dagger Rhys threatened to kill his arch-enemy. Devereux was not alone, his armed guard outnumbering Rhys and his men. With weapons drawn, it was not long before gestures and abuse changed into violent action. Scuffles and fighting broke out between the two arguing groups.

Rhys was overwhelmed and immediately disarmed. He was then sent off to the nearby Carmarthen Castle, the rest of his entourage either taking to their heels or finding themselves despatched to the rat-infested local prisons.

Catherine, wife of Rhys, was as dynamic as the Duke of Norfolk, her father, and quickly collected together the rest of the family retainers and supporters. These made up a force in the region of one hundred strong.

Catherine and her men promptly attacked Carmarthen Castle and while they were not able to free Rhys, several of Walter Devereux's men were killed in the assault. This was now much more than a mere brawl or riot. This was now open rebellion. Despite this, Henry remained blithely unaware of the problems – or if not aware content at least to allow Walter Devereux to control the problems in wild West Wales.

From where Henry sat the troubles in Wales were exactly that, mere troubles that Devereux, Lord Ferrers, as the man in charge, the commander on the spot, was expected to deal with and sort out. Over the next few weeks, Devereux tried his best. Events rumbled on, scuffles and the disruption of trade and commerce soon becoming the regular order of the day.

In an attempt to keep the peace, Rhys was eventually released from captivity but the bad blood between him and Devereux continued. Knife and sword fights in the streets of Carmarthen were soon matched by several episodes of piracy. Operating out of the Pembrokeshire port of Tenby, Rhys and his followers boarded ships sailing up the Bristol Channel and helped themselves to goods that were clearly meant for government or Devereux sources. It was lucrative and it infuriated the Ferrers regime.

It was a time of chaos and confusion, of blood and anger. Small wonder that Wales had once again become a land where 'the King's writ doth not run'.

Finally, as fear began to grow regarding what he and his supporters might do next, Rhys was arrested again, placed first in Carmarthen Castle and then transferred to London. The exact date of his transfer is unknown but he was certainly 'in residence' at the Tower by the beginning of 1531.

The matter had clearly passed beyond the control of Walter Devereux. It was now the king's problem. When the arrogant Rhys decided to add the title Fitz-Urien to his name, Henry began to worry even more. Was this a sign that Rhys was attempting to assert himself and create another government in Wales? It certainly looked like it. Urien was the ancient Welsh ruler of Rheged, a mythical but highly significant figure to the Welsh.

Rumours began to circulate that Rhys had been in contact with James V, King of Scotland, with a view to forming an alliance – although how this was possible when the Welshman had spent much of the last few years in close captivity remains a mystery. The rumour machine in operation again?

The idea of a Scottish-Welsh assault on his kingdom was enough for Henry, however, and on 4 December 1531 he took the easy way out. Rhys ap Gruffydd was executed for treason.

The execution caused widespread dismay in Wales. Many Welsh people thought Rhys was arrogant and too full of his own self-importance but could not bring themselves to believe that he was guilty of treason. Some took the opposite view, claiming that the fate of Rhys was nothing if not justified:

Many men regarded his death as Divine retribution for the falsehoods of his ancestors, his grandfather and great grandfather, and for their oppressions and wrongs. They had many a deep curse from the poor people who were their neighbours, for depriving them of their homes, lands and riches.[1]

Still others saw it as an act of judicial murder and Henry's desire to centralise government. Ralph Griffiths, who wrote the official history of the Thomas/Gruffydd family believed that the execution was based on charges that were devised to suit the prevailing domestic and political situation at the time – in other words, the king's desire to annul his marriage, to wed Anne Boleyn and bring about the eventual break with Rome.[2]

Others saw a more direct mercenary motive behind what they perceived as a set-up job. Certainly by 1531 Rhys and his family were in possession of huge amounts of land across Wales. By executing Rhys as a traitor, that land was forfeited to the Crown. The king was always short of money and selling off these estates brought in considerable wealth for Henry. If that was, indeed, the motive behind the execution, then it was, in many respects, a forerunner of the Dissolution of the Monasteries.

Only a few short years after the execution of Rhys ap Gruffydd, Henry's 1536 Act of Union united Wales and England. Power now really did exist only in London and any potential threat from Wales was, for the time being at least, extinguished. It is difficult to know what Rhys would have thought about that.

*   *   *

If the primary cause of the Welsh 'uprising' had been the arrogance and stupidity of one man, the same might also be said of a somewhat more serious Irish rebellion that erupted in 1534 and lasted for three long years.

The twenty-one-year-old Lord Thomas Fitzgerald was known throughout Ireland as Silken Thomas on account of the glorious trappings and accoutrements he wore. He was something of a 'Tudor dandy', laughed at by many, envied by others but always the perfect target for those who saw him as a naïve and totally inexperienced representative of English control.

In 1534 a group of Thomas's enemies – and there were many of them, both in Dublin and in the country beyond the Pale – began to spread the rumour that Thomas's father, Gerald Fitzgerald, Earl of Kildare, had been imprisoned and executed by the king. More than that, the rumour declared, Henry was next coming for Thomas himself.

In an age when communications between Ireland and London could well take weeks, such things were possible. Gerald Fitzgerald had, indeed, gone to England, summoned by the king to answer various charges of disorderly conduct. He had led an adventurous life, regularly taking up arms against his chief rival the Earl of Ossory and against other Irish nobles but there was never any suggestion of rebellion against the Crown.

On his departure for London Gerald Fitzgerald, then Lord Deputy of Ireland, appointed his son Thomas to act as deputy in his absence. The preening Silken Thomas seized on the opportunity to parade his position as the king's representative in Ireland. Then came the rumour of his father's execution.

Gerald Fitzgerald was, in fact, not dead at all but languishing in the Tower of London. He had not been executed or even charged at that stage but the wildly impressionable Silken Thomas chose to believe the worst. The king had killed his father, there was only one thing to do:

Vengeance, vengeance on the perjured and blood-guilty king, whose crimes of lust, murder and sacrilege called aloud for punishment, and forfeited for him allegiance, throne and life.[3]

With a small body of his cronies, all vividly attired and well-armed, Thomas rode for Dublin. The faster he rode the angrier he became with the result that when he finally entered the Council Chamber in St Mary's Abbey he was in a fury of self-righteous anger. The first thing that he did was to renounce his allegiance to the king.

Archbishop Cromer, primate of Armagh and a friend of both Fitzgerald and his son Thomas, pleaded with him not to be so foolish and for a while, the young dandy was swayed.

Then, one of Thomas's followers shouted that he should not forget that he was there to avenge his father. Within minutes the highly impressionable Thomas changed his stance and position yet again. He threw away the Sword of State and rushed out, followed by his supporters. The Silken Thomas Rebellion had begun.

Once out of the Council Chamber and undoubtedly urged on by his more reckless companions Thomas began gathering together a large body of troops and disaffected Irishmen. Such argumentative and violent men were always available on the fringes of Irish society. Now, having engaged their services by stressing the possibility of loot and plunder, Thomas led them back to the walls of Dublin.

The city had recently been weakened by an outbreak of plague and the inhabitants quailed before the approach of the Silken Thomas and his forces. They opened the gates and let them in. Thomas, in a moment of magnanimity, promised that he would look after the occupants of the town.

The immediate problem was not Dublin, however, but its castle where many of the leading citizens, Archbishop John Allen among them, had taken refuge. Allen was yet another leading individual who had fallen out with the Fitzgeralds.

He had been appointed Archbishop of Dublin and Lord Chancellor of Ireland by Thomas Wolsey, mainly with the idea of undermining the power of the Fitzgeralds. He would, Wolsey intended, embarrass the Fitzgeralds and make a thorough nuisance of himself.

In 1532 the ploy rebounded on Wolsey when Gerald Fitzgerald deprived Allen of the Chancellorship and whatever easy co-existence might have been achieved between the two men promptly dissolved. Now, while Thomas arranged his forces around the castle, Archbishop Allen decided that escape from Dublin was his only chance of survival.

Allen managed to slip out through the Dame Gate but his ship found itself stranded at Clantarf. Allen was forced to seek refuge in the house of a certain Mr Hollywood and there, on 28 July 1534, Silken Thomas caught up with him.

The archbishop was dragged from the house and in fear for his life fell on his knees, begging for mercy. Thomas was disgusted and muttered 'Take away the churl.' Archbishop Allen was immediately clubbed to death. Thomas was later to claim that his words had been misinterpreted, deliberately or accidentally he was never sure, but either way, the dye was now cast and there was no going back.

Almost before he knew it Thomas found himself at the head of a full-scale insurrection. Despite being excommunicated following the death of Archbishop Allen, powerful Irish chieftains immediately flocked to his standard. Their names read like a litany of Irish nobility – O'Carroll, O'Neill, and O'Brien to name just three.

Having been propelled into leading a major rebellion, Silken Thomas allowed himself to dream and develop aims that had certainly not been there at the outbreak of hostilities. He declared his rebellion to be a 'Catholic Crusade' and announced that his intention was to bring Ireland back under the sway of the true church. The people of Ireland should pledge obedience to the Pope rather than Henry VIII. 'Free Ireland' was now the call.

That winter, as the new Lord Deputy Sir William Skeffington sat inactive, Silken Thomas and Brian O'Connor, his new closest ally, invaded Meath, burning Trim, Dunboyne and much of the surrounding land. The English enclave around Dublin, known as the Pale, was depopulated as people fled in terror. For a brief moment, it really did seem as if a totally independent Irish kingdom might be established.

In March 1535, however, Skeffington finally lumbered into action and laid siege to Maynooth Castle, the most powerful of the Fitzgerald fortresses. Skeffington might have been inactive to start but now he quickly displayed his strength.

Despite being defended by several hundred soldiers, Maynooth Castle was battered by artillery fire and then stormed. After nine days the Great Keep, a bastion of immense size and strength, was the only part of the fortress that remained in rebel hands.

Eventually, the final thirty-seven defenders in the keep surrendered. According to the rules of warfare, they expected Skeffington to grant them mercy. All thirty-seven were promptly executed. The fall of Maynooth Castle and the execution of the last defenders put a dampener on the spirit of Thomas's men, even his great friend O'Moore of Leix abandoning him and heading for the sanctuary of home.

Within a few months, nearly three quarters of Kildare and Meath had been burned by English forces and, to make matters worse, plague broke out across the country. When Lord Leonard Grey became Marshal of Ireland and head of all military forces, he made swift work of whatever rebel resistance remained. The heart had gone from the revolt.

Thomas and Brian O'Connor saw no alternative but to send Lord Grey an offer of submission. It was readily received. O'Connor was pardoned but Silken Thomas was immediately taken into captivity and sent off to England to await punishment.

He spent the next eighteen months languishing in what was, for him, the greatest possible misery. True to his character, when given paper to write a letter he produced not an explanation for his deeds but a request for money in order to buy clothes:

> I never had any money since I came into prison, but a noble, nor have I hosen, doublet or shoes, nor shirt but one; nor any other garment but a single frieze gown ... and so I have gone shoeless and barefoot and barelegged divers (sic) times while it hath not been very warm; and so I should have done still but that poor prisoners of their gentleness hath sometimes given me old hosen and shoes and shirts.[4]

The letter was sent to an old servant along with the request that he should contact O'Brien, Earl of Thomond, to ask for a gift of £20. While Silken Thomas was lamenting his lack of shoes and shirts, five of his uncles – at least three of whom had little to do with the rebellion – were executed at Tyburn.

Ironically Silken Thomas had become Earl of Kildare early on in his rebellion. The stories about the execution of his father might have been lies but Thomas's revolt caused the old man such grief that on 12 December 1534, just a few days after receiving news of the rising, he took to his bed and died. That immediately elevated Thomas into the position of 10th Earl of Kildare.

The Act of Attainder allowing the execution of Silken Thomas went through Parliament late in 1536 and on 3 February 1537 he was beheaded on Tower Green. In the wake of the Silken Thomas Rebellion all of the Fitzgerald titles and holdings were forfeited and many members of the Fitzgerald clan were forced to seek shelter in Europe.

Only in the reign of the Catholic Queen Mary, long after Henry was dead and buried, was the 11th Earl of Kildare allowed to reclaim his ancestral rights and honours. In the meantime, Henry and his subjects could well do without the type of dissension and disturbance created by one arrogant and self-interested nobleman.

Allowing the Fitzgeralds to once more claim and use the title of Earls of Kildare was to be expected. Mary – Bloody Mary as she was later dubbed – brought back the Catholic faith to England and with it, the fires of over 300 heretical victims were lit. Giving back the Fitzgerald holdings was, in contrast, small beer for the daughter of Henry VIII!

If nothing else the Silken Thomas rebellion had alerted Henry to conditions in Ireland and in 1541, partly as a result of Henry's desire for strong central control and partly because of Thomas Fitzgerald's activities, the Kingdom of Ireland was established. All of his life the king feared uprising and revolt and the Irish were happy to give it to him.

The whole affair had cost Henry somewhere in the region of £75,000 to suppress the rebellion – an astronomical sum of money for that time; he was not going to make the same mistake again.

Chapter Nine

The Break with Rome, Monasteries Included

Henry VIII was a driven man, urged onwards by two significant desires, both rampant but not necessarily conflicting urges – the need to secure a son and heir, and a recurring passion to enjoy the pleasures of the flesh. Together they produced the English Reformation and the irreparable break with Rome.

Even as early as 1520 it was clear that Catherine of Aragon was never going to provide Henry with the male heir he so desperately wanted. During their marriage, she had given birth to just one healthy child, the Princess Mary, all of her other six children having been stillborn or dying a few days after entering the world. By 1525 she had stopped menstruating and Henry was faced with the prospect of his only child, a girl, succeeding to the throne after him.

The idea of that filled Henry with dread. The last time a woman had sat on the throne there had been chaos in the country. That had been the Empress Matilda, several hundred years before, and then civil war had plagued England for over twenty years.

A much closer example of what might happen in the reign of a weak monarch was available for him in the Wars of the Roses. Then the floundering ruler had been King Henry VI rather than a woman but the message was still the same – weakness equalled disharmony and chaos. Henry was determined that there would be no return to either of those examples of internal civil conflict.

Gradually he became convinced – or, more likely, convinced himself – that his marriage to Catherine was cursed. God was punishing him, he felt, by failing to provide him with a healthy male heir. The marriage to Catherine should never have been permitted and he had his proof in two verses from the Bible:

Thou shalt not uncover the nakedness of thy brother's wife ... If a man shall take his brother's wife, it is an unclean thing ... they shall be childless.[1]

Henry had recently fathered a son with his mistress, Elizabeth Blount. It was proof positive, in his eyes at least, that there was nothing wrong with his fertility or his ability to father a male child. Therefore, lack of a formal male heir had to be divine intervention and the fault of the woman with whom he had effectively been living in sin for many years!

Catherine, previously wife to Henry's brother Arthur, was adamant that due to his poor health her first marriage to Arthur had never been consummated. It was possible although there had never been any sort of examination of Catherine's body. Henry's father and Henry himself wanted the marriage at all costs and in 1502 after the death of Arthur, the Pope had granted dispensation for the new couple, Catherine and Henry, to be wed. They were immediately betrothed and married seven years later when he became king.

No matter how eager Henry had been to marry Catherine in 1509, he was now much keener to be rid of her. He appealed to the new Pope, Clement VII, to declare the marriage null and void. In other words, he wanted an annulment.

While he waited for a response from the Pope, Henry suggested that Catherine should retire to a nunnery. She knew that the country needed a strong male heir, it was the least she could do for him and for England, he declared. It was hardly a humane or politic request and Catherine refused. She was the Queen of England and Henry's loyal wife; she would stay by his side and do her duty. Henry understood but not for one moment did he accept her decision. Everything, now, depended on Pope Clement VII delivering his judgement.

The mood of the people was one of unhappiness. Many were downright truculent. Catherine had always been popular, appealing to the romantic element of society. Widowed young, beautiful to look at, spirited and brave in times of crisis like the Scottish invasion of 1513, she was everything the people could ever want. It was just unfortunate that Henry did not feel the same.

Catherine of Aragon was banished from court, given the title of Dowager Princess of Wales – in view of her previous marriage to Arthur – and exiled to Kimbolton Castle where she lived out her days. Whenever she appeared in public, which was not often, she was cheered and applauded to the echo. Whenever her replacement Anne Boleyn appeared in London, something which happened much more often, she was hissed and booed all the way down the street.

Meanwhile, the campaign for an annulment continued. William Knight, one of the king's chief secretaries, was despatched by Cardinal Wolsey to Rome in order to plead Henry's case. It was unfortunate for Knight that politics and warfare promptly and perhaps inevitably got in the way of an easy answer to the King's difficulty.

In 1527 as part of the ongoing conflict between France, Spain and the Holy Roman Empire the forces of Charles V, the Emperor, had attacked and sacked the city of Rome. The Pope had managed to escape from the Vatican through a secret tunnel and took refuge in the Castel Saint Angelo. There he was holed up, hardly able to move, little more than a 'puppet Pope' in the hands of Charles.

When Knight arrived in Rome, he was denied easy access to Pope Clement and spent several troubling days trying to reach his quarry. He did eventually meet the Pope and even managed to obtain a 'conditional dispensation' to bring back to Henry. Knight was delighted with his success but Wolsey immediately declared that it was not enough. Knight retired from the fray, probably thinking 'If you can do better, go and do it yourself!'

Wolsey, of course, decided that he certainly could do better. And Henry agreed. Now the solution to *The King's Great Matter* rested solely with his loyal minister, Cardinal Thomas Wolsey. Henry had faith in his Lord Chancellor but even at the beginning of the enterprise Wolsey knew it would be a difficult task.

Charles V was the nephew of Catherine and he had no desire to see his aunt cast aside. In the world of sixteenth-century politics, Henry's dilemma was a great bargaining piece and at Charles's direction, the captive Clement refused to grant an annulment to the English King.

Wolsey's response was to have Clement convene an ecclesiastical court in England. The Papal delegate, Cardinal Lorenzo Campeggio, was not a well man, suffering from gout and other ailments. His health was so bad that he had to make many stops to supposedly rest and recuperate on his journey to England. He was two months late in arriving and, when he did appear, seemed reluctant to make a decision – hardly surprising when he was under orders from Clement and Charles not to make any firm rulings or agreements.

Eventually, the game having been played to its conclusion, Campeggio was recalled by the Pope. In 1529 the court, which had been attended by both Henry and Catherine, one pleading for an annulment, the other offering a tearful acknowledgement of her duty and role, was suspended. It had been unable to come to any sort of a decision.

Pope Clement now declared that Henry should not involve himself in a new marriage until the matter of the annulment was solved. And it should be solved not in England but in Rome. The matter, it seemed, was going round and round, getting precisely nowhere.

Wolsey had failed his master in finding a solution to *The King's Great Matter* and he was to be the first significant victim in the affair. Anne Boleyn had always believed that Wolsey's loyalties lay with the Pope rather than Henry and she was not afraid to give vent to her feelings – more whisperings in the king's ear!

Inevitably, Wolsey was dismissed and told it would be 'politic' if he went north, to the centrepiece of his bishopric at York. This Wolsey now did, the first time he had ever been near to his See, the land he supposedly governed as Archbishop of York.

If Wolsey was expecting a pleasant or easy retirement then he was gravely mistaken. Henry's vengeance followed him. Unfortunately for the cardinal Henry now uncovered a written suggestion from Wolsey to the Pope suggesting that as a way forward Anne Boleyn might perhaps be sent into exile? It was a blow to the solar plexus for the king who had always trusted Wolsey implicitly and his temper exploded into violent rage.

Wolsey was called back to London where he would undoubtedly find himself facing charges of treason. Wolsey was apparently greatly distressed by the news and by Henry's summons but obediently set off for London. He never made it, forestalling his king's vengeance by dying, probably from a heart attack brought on by severe dysentery, at Leicester on 29 November 1530.

*   *   *

During all of the negotiations and secret dealings, Anne Boleyn had sat and fretted. She knew that Henry was in love with her but, according to legend, for nearly seven years she had managed to keep him at arm's length.

The story of Henry's infatuation with Anne Boleyn is well known. Kings were expected to take mistresses but this was different, this was total and utter carnal desire on the part of Henry. Anne was not the most beautiful of women but her personality was lively and compelling. That made her a target for Henry's lust. But in Anne, the king had met his match.

She would sleep with him, she declared, only when Catherine was removed from the picture and when there was more of a future for her than being just another mistress of the king, easily picked up and easily disposed of. She had seen how Henry had dropped her sister Mary when she no longer pleased him and she was certainly not going to allow the same fate to befall her.

How true the story of the seven years wait really was remains, now, difficult to appreciate. It seems impossible, given the nature of the Tudor court, that Anne did not relent at some stage and take Henry to her bed. But she was a superb player of the courtly love rules and certainly for a long while she managed to retain her chastity, at least as far as Henry was concerned.

Both Henry and Anne were fascinated by the concept of courtly love. It was a process of wooing, of obedience to the lady's slightest command and of flirting in words and actions. Courtly love derived from medieval authors like Andreas Capellanus and from the famous *Morte d'Arthur* of Thomas Mallory which appeared in 1485, the year of Bosworth Field and the founding of the Tudor dynasty. In the annals of courtly love, chastity was always preferable to consummation so perhaps Anne did after all manage to keep Henry at bay for those long years of waiting.

Courtly love became almost a way of life for the king and his would-be wife. And it was not just Henry and Anne. Indeed, the whole of Henry's court was intrigued by the idea of 'acting out the fantasy of love'.[2]

On its own, however, courtly love could not last forever. In order to survive, it needed substance of some sort, backing that would enable Anne to see where the affair was heading. She was an ambitious woman who needed to see that there was a future for her and the king. That was soon to arrive, with a little help from Henry and his courtiers.

When Archbishop Warham died in October 1532, Henry immediately put his own man in place as the most senior cleric in the country. Thomas Cranmer, the Boleyn family's chaplain, was installed in Warham's position as the new Archbishop of Canterbury – and Cranmer was malleable enough to help the king find a solution to the affair.

The same year Thomas Cromwell, the new advisor and 'Mr Fix It' for the king, ensured the beginning of the break with Rome when he forced through Parliament what is now known as the Submission of the Clergy.

Included in this Submission was the statement that the clergy would pass no new laws without permission of the monarch. A review of existing laws, undertaken by the king, would also take place and Convocation would not be called without the express permission of – you've guessed it – the king. Supremacy of the monarchy over the church had been established.

The Act of Supremacy, declaring Henry to be Supreme Head of the Church in England, soon followed in 1534. All of this was enough to secure Cromwell's position as Lord Privy Seal and therefore the chief minister to the Crown and to the state. It would also ensure the execution of men like Thomas More and John Fisher, regrettable perhaps but unlikely to hold up matters for too long.

With Henry now declared Supreme Head of the Church in England, he was free to interpret the sanctity and relevance of his first marriage in any way he liked. And, of course, he was able to court Anne in whatever way he felt appropriate.

Anne Boleyn was being seen in public with Henry more and more, at official and unofficial meetings, or glimpsed in private at one or the other of the king's palaces – much to the anger of the English people. Indeed, by the end of 1532, she was living openly with the king in Greenwich. Things were about to escalate to the next level.

Anne accompanied Henry to Calais for a meeting with Francis and on the way back, on 14 November 1532 in Dover she and the king were secretly married. With Anne clearly pregnant a formal marriage took place on 25 January 1533.

On 23 May 1533 Archbishop Cranmer, at a specially convened court in the convent at Dunstable, declared the marriage of Henry and Catherine to be invalid. Cranmer and the king had chosen the location well.

Dunstable was hardly the most public of places and the announcement went off without any intervention or objection from the king's subjects, something that Henry and his advisors had feared might happen. Five days later Cranmer ruled that the marriage between Henry and Catherine was entirely lawful.

Catherine of Aragon lingered only a little while after Henry married Anne. She died on 7 January 1536 from the unusual affliction of cancer of the heart. On the day of her death, Anne Boleyn miscarried a baby boy.

With the death of Catherine, public dislike of Anne Boleyn reached a new level, not helped by the fact that the new queen wore a yellow dress rather than the traditional black during the official mourning period. The fact that Henry also wore yellow was conveniently forgotten. But then, yellow was the traditional Spanish mourning colour and in Henry, it was viewed simply as a case of showing respect. With Anne, it was an insult! The people fumed but could do very little.

*   *   *

Henry had, by the 1534 Act of Supremacy, taken for himself the power to control and discipline the clergy. He also obtained the right or duty to oversee canon law, included in which was the right to accuse and try heretics. More importantly, it gave him the right of visitation and inspection. In 1535 he delegated his powers – in ecclesiastical matters – to Thomas Cromwell when he appointed him Vicar General of the country.[3]

Thomas Cromwell, like Archbishop Cranmer, was always more of a Protestant than his master, the king. Henry remained, after all was said and done, a Catholic in everything but name. He despised the teachings of men like Luther and Calvin, viewing their activities on the continent with dark suspicion. He had even gone so far as to publish a book – probably half-written by Sir Thomas More – criticising Luther's proposed church reforms. The Pope awarded him the title *Fidei Defensor* (Defender of the Faith). That had been before the matter of an heir became a significant issue.

Cranmer's leanings towards a less orthodox style of religion were well known and his appointment as Archbishop of Canterbury signalled, for many Protestants, a clear move away from the rigours of the Catholic Church and the governance of the Bishop of Rome. His partnership with Thomas Cromwell meant that the duo at the apex of English political life were considerably more revolutionary in their views and religious practices than the king. At some stage, there would have to be a reckoning – but in 1536 that lay some distance in the future.

Protestantism was a faith or a creed that Thomas Cromwell had encountered during his time on the Continent but if he was going to bring it into England, in however small a way, he would have to be careful not to over-reach himself. It was a lesson he eventually forgot and his poor judgement in the acquisition of Henry's fourth wife, Anne of Cleves, was a contributing factor in his downfall. For the moment, though, Cromwell was content to play the long game.

Henry's traditionalist views were well known and, of course, he was unpredictable, needing careful handling over issues like religion. As ever, the perpetual whispers in the ear were the most successful way of dealing with a king like Henry who really did believe that every good idea was his, every misjudgement was the fault of his advisors.

There was one target that was readily available and with careful management, it was a target of which Henry was almost certain to approve. The monasteries of England and Wales had existed in splendid isolation for hundreds of years. Most of them were very rich and were generally international or continental in their approach to life.

The monasteries and convents were, in the main controlled by foreign Catholic orders based in France, Spain and Italy. Monks owed their allegiance, first, to the Pope and only then to the king. When the break with Rome occurred that made the loyalty of the monks at best questionable and in a few cases actually treasonable.

Between them Cromwell and Cranmer began to whet the king's appetite. The wealth, the land, the property of the monasteries, they suggested to him, would bring in thousands to the Royal Treasury and to Henry's own pocket. Dissolve the monasteries and all of it could be his!

At this early stage, the break with Rome had been relatively painless for the people. After all, the church services remained the same, readings from the Bible were still in the original Latin and all the trappings they were used to were in place. Wafts of incense, smoke from guttering candles, plainsong chanted by the priest – all that was different was that the head of the church was now Henry VIII, not the Pope, and that barely affected anyone.

A small band of intellectuals and thinkers, men like Bishop Fisher and Sir Thomas More, went to their deaths rather than accept Henry as a replacement for the Pope. They were in a minority, however. Most English men and women accepted the new, slightly tweaked status quo.

Cranmer and Cromwell were sure that the second stage of the break, the dissolution of the monasteries, would be the same. They totally misjudged the situation, as we shall see.

The dissolution of the monasteries could be cloaked up in whichever way Henry wanted but, at its root, there was only one reason behind this assault on one of the country's more seminal institutions – the chronic financial situation of the king and his style of ruling. It was a case of money, money, money!

Cranmer and Cromwell might mutter darkly about the doctrines of purgatory and idolatry, so beloved by the monks, so hated by Protestants, but that could not hide the relative poverty of the Crown. And it most certainly could not even begin to hide the massive reserve of wealth available in the religious houses.

There were by-products, as well, and that was where Cromwell excelled. He knew that he could, by selling monastic land at 'knock down' prices, bind the nobility of the country to the king. Traditionally truculent and full of their own importance, if he could ensure that the nobles owed Henry, owed him big time, it would go some way to ensuring peace in the land.

Cromwell could not admit this to the world, of course, and therefore he had to find excuses for closure of the religious houses. And in this, the monasteries and convents unknowingly helped him with almost self-destructive glee.

Beginning in 1534 he set up and organised a programme known as the Visitation of the Monasteries, supposedly an enquiry into the state of the finances and assets of the religious houses. As might be expected, visiting commissioners were soon claiming to have uncovered many examples of sexual immorality and financial irregularities amongst the monks and the nuns. It was, often, little more than a justification of their actions but the commissioners, working on the assumption that if you look long and hard enough you will always discover something untoward, did manage to come across many practices that were more than a little questionable.

Although monastic orders like the Benedictines and the Cistercians had sworn to abide quietly in remote and far-off locations where they could observe a life of poverty and obedience, the commissioners soon discovered that this was not always the case. Many monks lived in fine style, maybe not all of them but enough to justify the actions of Cromwell's commissioners.

Fine food served on silver platters, the best wines and ales available on the table, robes lined with ermine – there were more than a few instances of such indulgence uncovered during the investigations. At this distance, it is difficult to make judgements about the validity of the findings so that how much of it all was genuine and how much was the commissioners giving Cromwell and Cranmer what they wanted to hear remains unknown.

False relics, however, were regularly uncovered. These ranged from the supposed bones of saints to a vial of Christ's blood which, when examined, turned out to be a mixture of vinegar, wine and water. Henry, of course, was delighted with the findings.

In 1536 the Dissolution of the Lesser Monasteries Act was passed. Any monastery with less than £200 income a year was to be closed immediately. Even then, there was a get-out clause, temporary as it might be. Thirty-four houses were saved from closure by paying for exemption. Nobody questioned where the money came from.

Some monasteries, like the Franciscan Houses, closed their doors before Cromwell could actually get to them. This occurred in August 1534 after the Franciscan Order refused to accept the repudiation of Papal authority and withdrew from the country. Other religious orders fought to the bitter end.

The dissolution of the smaller monasteries and convents – *Valor Ecclesiasticus* (translated as 'the Value of the Church') – staggered Henry and brought him more wealth than he had ever dreamed possible. Between the implementation of the Act and his death eleven years later an enormous sum of over £1.5 million was put into the king's coffers. Inevitably, dissolution of the larger monasteries followed hot on the footsteps of the smaller, less well-known religious houses.

In total over 800 monasteries were disbanded and their land sold off during the process known as the Dissolution of the Monasteries. It was a time of disbelief as many of the priors and abbots sat serenely in splendid isolation, perhaps in shock, but certainly believing until the end that it could not happen to them.

Cromwell and Anne Boleyn had always maintained an uneasy peace between themselves, each seeing the mutual benefit that could be gained by co-operation. However, with the closure of the monasteries there came the first hint of discord.

Much to Cromwell's chagrin, Anne suggested that, rather than further enrich the wealthy by pouring money and land into their pockets, the monastery land and buildings should be used as places of study and as centres for continued relief of the poor. Her suggestion was ignored by Cromwell and, as a consequence, by the king as well.

Anne's philanthropic view has rarely been acknowledged by historians and interested parties who have preferred to see her as a self-interested, upwardly mobile good time girl. Even at the time, the ordinary peasants of the country, the people who would suffer most in the dissolution process, also failed to give her the credit she deserved. The land went to the wealthy.

However, from the first few instances of dissolution, there was growing opposition to the concept of closure. Monasteries and convents were, after all, places where the poor could receive sanctuary and help in times of trouble. The monks or the nuns were the closest things that Tudor England ever had to medical practitioners. Not only that, in many instances the larger monasteries provided much-needed employment:

> Monasteries were local employers and landlords. Many farmers leased land from the monks, and the monasteries also provided employment on their estates for both unskilled agricultural labourers and skilled craftsmen.[4]

Now this was all to be thrown out and the people reacted in the only way they knew. Mobs began to gather outside threatened monasteries, stones were thrown and attempts made to stop the entrance of Cromwell's officials to the religious houses.

In several instances, the Suppression Commissioners and workmen sent to pull down monastic buildings were threatened and then subjected to violence from men and women who were local to the area. Fights and fisticuffs between the local populace and the commissioners were not exactly common but they were not unknown either.

Cromwell had a huge target to aim for. By the time of Henry's accession to the throne, there were nearly 900 religious houses in England alone and somewhere in the region of 12,000 men and women serving in religious orders. If he was going to successfully purge the country of what he and Cranmer saw as centres of Catholic faith he needed help, skilled help from unscrupulous men, who would do his bidding without too many worries and doubts.

One such person was Sir Richard Rich, perhaps the most devious and self-seeking courtier he could find. Unscrupulous but efficient, Rich was made Chancellor of the Court of Augmentations just as the dissolutions were beginning. Perfect timing! It was Rich who managed the revenue from the closed down monasteries and in doing so he enriched both the Crown and himself![5]

Ordering the closure of a monastery was only the start of the process. Once everything had been put in place legally, the destruction would begin.

From 1536 onwards wholesale obliteration of monastic buildings added to the ecclesiastical destruction of the monastic system. What took place over the next dozen or so years was an orgy of vandalism on an enormous scale. Cromwell, Cranmer and Henry did not want anything that could be used by disruptive elements in society – beggars, vandals, out of work monks – to be left standing. There was to be nothing left where people could gain access or help themselves to shelter.

Consequently, lead was stripped from the monastery rooves, melted down and made into such things as enormous drinking troughs for cattle. No lead on the roof meant that rainwater poured into the buildings with the result that walls and columns which had stood proudly for years soon crumbled and fell.

Walls and doors were smashed and sometimes fires were started by using curtains and bedding as fuel. Stained glass windows, delicate works of art that had survived for centuries, were smashed out of their frames, trampled on and crushed into millions of pieces.

Monasteries had always been centres of learning and from earliest Christian times monks had been responsible for copying and preserving old books. Come the dissolution, if these had not been carried away by the more perceptive abbot or other senior monastery officials when the place received notification of closure, they were simply ripped up and burned by the commissioners. It was destruction on a grand scale.

Objections to the closures had been local affairs. Feelings had run high, Henry was informed, but once the monastery or convent had been closed the emotions of the people subsided quickly enough. Or did they?

For the first time, worries began to circulate about just how far this wanton destruction would be allowed to go. Would their own parish churches be next, people asked? There was no answer and in the vacuum that was created by that lack of response, fear grew rapidly. The next stage would be open rebellion.

Chapter Ten

The Pilgrimage of Grace – Before, During and After

If, to begin with, Henry was pleased at how relatively peaceful his break with Rome had been, there was a rude awakening hovering in the background, just waiting to strike. Henry and Cranmer had, as they expected, been excommunicated by the Pope and while the king's subjects had not taken kindly to his new queen it was a momentary displeasure, Henry felt sure. In time it would, like all bad things, pass into history and be forgotten.

If Henry was greatly disturbed by his excommunication, he did not seem to let it worry him unduly. By discounting the relevance of the Pope as God's representative on earth he had reduced the Vicar of Rome to the position of an also-ran. He, Henry, was now Supreme Head of the Church in England, let the Pope rant and rave all he liked. It hardly mattered.

Henry's immortal soul was one thing, something to be dealt with later, but his chief concern, one that could not be shunted onto a back burner, had always been that Charles V might intervene, might even launch an invasion of England. As it happened, the threat had come to nothing. Now, with Cromwell at the helm, money was beginning to pour into the royal coffers from the sale of monastic land and property. It all seemed to be going to plan.

And then things started to go wrong. Within weeks of the first monastery closure, the process of dissolution came under attack. The disorder around Henry's dissolution of the monasteries has since come to be viewed as something of a catalyst, an ulcer or a cancer eating away at the very structure of his brave new world – at the time it was seen as a minor irritation that could be easily swept away. It was a surface problem that meant little but, when looked at closely, the disturbances were symbolic of far deeper concerns than the mere closure of religious houses.

The first objections came, naturally enough, from the clergy and that was a problem that surfaced even before the troubles around the dissolutions began to be felt. They came as the pace of the 'English Reformation' began to pick up.

The first of the Henrician Injunctions, accompanied by the Ten Articles of the new Anglican Church, were put into practice in the summer of 1536. By the terms of these new laws the concept of Purgatory and the observance of holy days – somewhere between forty and fifty each year – were totally rejected. And that brought problems that Henry had never considered:

> Purgatory and prayers for the dead had been a central tenet of the medieval Church and were woven into the fabric of local religious culture, which also set great store by the veneration of local saints and pilgrimages.[1]

Despite having been approved by Convocation, albeit a Henry-controlled Convocation, many local priests were adamant that they would not accept the new rulings. To almost everyone at that time Heaven, Hell and Purgatory were not abstract concepts but real places and the priests were representatives of such beliefs. The remoter the parish, the more reluctant the priests seemed to be to embrace the changes. It was a classic case of the head and the heart going off in different directions.

In the summer of 1536, a Dorset Priest called Lovell was reported for what was called 'disloyal preaching', encouraging people to observe the prohibited holy days and to light candles as part of the service. In September 1536, despite the Injunctions, the curates of several Hertfordshire parishes kept the holy days with the ringing of bells and continual singing. Cromwell and Anne Boleyn were denounced in the Abbey at St Albans. And so on – and so on![2] There were many more examples of priests going their own way.

From what had appeared to Henry to be a more or less amicable acceptance of the religious changes the situation had drastically altered within a few brief months. And then came the dissolution of the monasteries. It was the spark that triggered not only disaffection but open rebellion.

On 4 October 1536 the first rebellion broke out in Lincolnshire. Ostensibly an objection to the closure of the local monastery, when looked at objectively it was clear that this rebellion was also a sign of discontent at the general direction of Henry's religious changes.

Discontent flared into violence when Dr Raynes, Chancellor of the Bishop of Lincoln, arrived in the town of Louth to carry out a visitation of the clergy. Only a few years before the Church of St James in Louth had acquired a new spire. The local people were proud of their spire and of their church and, hearing that Raynes was coming, were afraid of what he might say or do. Nearby Louth Park Abbey had been recently visited by commissioners and had been immediately closed down. Was Raynes about to do the same with their church?

Fearful of what Raynes might do, on the evening of 4 October a group of local men and women armed themselves and mounted a night-long vigil over the church. When, the following morning, Raynes appeared outside the church, it was a signal for tempers to flare. He was dragged from his horse by the tired but angry townspeople but at this stage, nobody quite knew what to do with the captured man and his retinue.

The Louth protesters decided they would march to nearby Legbourne Convent where Cromwell's commissioners were already at work, pulling down the building and stripping it of its assets. A confrontation or fracas between the two groups flared up, resulting in one of the commissioners, a man called Thomas Wulcey, being killed.

When the mob marched on to Horncastle anger again spilt over. The Louth mob was met by a large contingent of men and women from the Horncastle area. Amongst the crowd were many priests, vocal in their objection to the monastery closures and religious changes.

To cries of 'Kill him, kill him!' Dr Raynes was again pulled from his horse, this time by two men named William Hutchinson and William Bolderstone. He was then forced to his knees and, as mass hysteria and mob violence took over, beaten to death.

At this point, the more realistic members of the uprising decided that rather than continue to rampage through the country what they needed to do was make an appeal to the king. There had already been two deaths, both of them church and government officials – and that was two deaths too many. Trusting the king's benevolence, the leaders of the rising decided they would send him a petition outlining their grievances.

The most significant of their complaints was the closure of the monasteries but the Lincolnshire rebels did not stop there. Heavy taxation in the form of subsidies and the old issue of enclosures were also highlighted in their petition. So too was the comment, injudicious as it might be, that the king seemed to be promoting men of low birth, notably Thomas Cromwell and Sir Richard Rich, into positions of high authority. From these men, the king was receiving 'evil counsel'.

Having written and despatched their petition, the rebels marched on again. This time their destination was Lincoln. By now they had been joined by men from Market Rasen and Caistor, the host numbering well in excess of 10,000 men and women. The local nobles, Lord Hussey and Lord Clinton, who should have dealt with the situation, had already fled and the rebel 'army' settled down on Hambledon Hill outside Lincoln to await the king's reply.

What made the Lincolnshire Rising unusual was that it encompassed a wide cross-section of society. It had begun with peasants and traders but quickly grew to include members of the clergy, fearful of losing their livings, and several representatives of the local gentry. The gentry, most of whom were JP's and magistrates, were later to claim that they had joined the rebellion simply in order to ensure it did not become too violent. The claim might have had some substance but now, with distance, it does seem a little disingenuous.

The acknowledged leader of the protest was a shoemaker from Louth, a man by the name of Nicholas Melton. Perhaps inevitably, given his profession, he soon became known to everyone as Captain Cobbler!

Melton/Cobbler had gained the affection of the mob in the early stage of the affair when he had grabbed one of the commissioners' registers, set it on fire and brandished it in front of the man's face. Captain Cobbler was closely advised by Thomas Kendall, the Vicar of Louth, who had sparked off the disaffection with an inflammatory sermon a week earlier, and by many others of both high and low station in life.

By 10 October a royalist army under the Duke of Suffolk had been despatched by the king and had reached Stamford, some forty or fifty miles away from Lincoln. Ahead of the army came heralds with the reply from Henry and it was clear that the king was not in the mood to forgive or forget:

I never have read, heard nor known that princes' counsellors and prelates should be appointed by rude and ignorant common people; nor that they were persons meet or of ability to discern and choose meet and sufficient counsellors for a prince. How presumptuous are ye, the rude commons of one shire, and that one of the most brute and beastly of the whole realm and of least experience, to find fault in your prince for the electing of his counsellors and prelates.[3]

Henry's reply to the petition concluded with the comment that the only religious houses earmarked to be closed were ones that were filled with vice and corruption. Then came the threat, slightly veiled but backed up by the menacing approach of Suffolk and his troops – go back to your homes and stay there.

The response of their king to what had seemed a reasonable petition and request knocked the heart out of the Lincolnshire rebels. Captain Cobbler and the other leaders were men who believed in the structure of society with the king at the top, dispensing justice as he saw fit. And he had clearly seen fit to ignore their requests.

Despite the fact that the rebel force had now increased to over 20,000, there was to be no pitched battle. Faced by Suffolk and his professional soldiers most of the rebels slipped quietly away, heading back to their homes before battle could begin, and the rebellion ended as quickly and as unceremoniously as it began.

By 11 October it was all over. The members of the gentry threw themselves on the mercy of the Duke of Suffolk and asked for pardon for their actions. That left men like Nicholas Melton, the infamous Captain Cobbler, and Thomas Kendall, the Louth priest, to face justice on their own. Over 100 of the more serious offenders were rounded up, tried and convicted of treason.

Most of them were duly hanged, notable victims including Captain Cobbler, who had earned the gratitude of the people by his leadership and unstinting loyalty to the rebellion. It was loyalty that was to last until the end, one of his final spoken words from the condemned cell being about the perfidy of the gentry:

What whoresons we were that we had not killed the gentlemen for I thought always that they would be traytours.[4]

Also executed was Thomas Kendall, the Vicar of Louth, who was hanged, drawn and quartered. Most of the gentry got away scot-free.

*   *   *

The Pilgrimage of Grace erupted in the second week of October 1536, just as the Lincolnshire Rising was coming to an end. It began at Beverley in the East Riding of Yorkshire and while similar to the events unfolding in Lincolnshire, it was a separate event.

There had been some communication between disaffected men in Yorkshire and those in Lincoln and, at one stage, the Lincoln rebels believed that disaffected Yorkshire protesters were coming to join them. That obviously did not happen but it showed the levels of dissatisfaction and unrest in the northern parts of the country.

Under the leadership of lawyer Robert Aske, close to 10,000 northern insurgents gathered together to vent their displeasure at the religious changes occurring in the country. On 21 October 1536 they besieged and captured Skipton Castle. Lord Darcy promptly surrendered nearby Pontefract Castle and joined the rebels.

York, the second largest and most important city in England at that time, was the next target for members of the Pilgrimage of Grace. With very little effort they stormed and also took the city which was poorly defended. They then proceeded to reclaim many of the forfeited church properties and restore some of the expelled Catholic monks and nuns to their religious houses in the city.

Robert Aske now issued a public proclamation stating the peaceful intentions of his rebels but stressing and emphasising their fervent desire to protect the Catholic Church – or, as he saw it, the only church!

The name Pilgrimage of Grace had been co-opted by Aske, the term seeming to him to catch the essential religious element in the uprising. Those who took part really did believe they were on a pilgrimage rather than engaging in open rebellion and referred to themselves as Pilgrims. Participants swore an oath to The Honourable Men, as the leaders called themselves, the oath being taken over the Bible and considered binding for all time:

Ye shall not enter into this our Pilgrimage of Grace for the common wealth but only for the love ye bear to God's faith and church militant and the maintenance thereof, the preservation of the king's person, his issue, and the purifying of the nobility and to expulse all villein blood and evil counsellors against the common wealth of the same. And ye shall not enter into our said pilgrimage for no particular private profit.[5]

Importantly, the causes of the Pilgrimage of Grace were not just religious ones. There were economic and social reasons that were significant for all levels of society.

Economically it had been a disastrous time for farmers and peasants all over the country but particularly in the northern shires. The poor harvest of 1535 had led to astronomically high food prices while the proposed dissolution of the monasteries wiped out the only succour and help that the poorer members of society could find. Two of the demands of the Pilgrims were a reduction in taxes to take account of this and an end to monastery closures.

There were also a wide range of what could be termed political causes. The men of the north disliked the way Henry had treated his wife Catherine of Aragon. While they had no love for Anne Boleyn, they were conscious that the recent charges leading to her trial and execution were clearly trumped-up and that was something, it was felt, which undermined the prestige and standing of the monarchy. The base-born Thomas Cromwell and his acolytes like Richard Rich were anathema to them and they demanded that Henry drop both of them immediately.

From a religious point of view, the church was the centre of community life and the peasants were worried that this support was about to be removed. Not only that, with the well-known Protestant dislike of idolatry and pageant it was feared that the plate and candles of their churches might be confiscated. There were even rumours that baptisms were going to be taxed. The Pilgrims wanted the old Catholic service and religion restored.

Arguably, the greatest mistake the Pilgrims made was not to march on London but to stay in the north. They placed their faith in the king and rather than head en masse for the capital they compiled a petition expressing their grievances, certain that Henry would deal with them fairly and honourably. It was duly presented to the king's representatives.

Robert Aske, conscious of his position and place as a middle-class lawyer, offered leadership of the Pilgrimage to the local nobleman Thomas Davey. Davey refused the leadership but did arrange for flags and banners to be made, to be carried by the Pilgrims as they marched. The banners were little works of art, showing the five wounds of Christ and reinforcing the religious aspect of the uprising. With Davey refusing leadership Aske saw no alternative but to retain it for himself.

Henry's initial reaction to the demands of the Pilgrims was one of anger and he immediately despatched the Duke of Norfolk to put down the rebellion. By the end of October, the Duke had reached Newark-on-Trent.

Cromwell, however, realising that this uprising was far more serious than the Lincolnshire affair now counselled caution. Delaying tactics, he told the king, would be better than direct action which would only lead to bloodshed on both sides. Norfolk, when he arrived in the north to find himself facing a well-organised rebel army of over 40,000 armed men, totally agreed. He was significantly outnumbered and like all good generals knew when to fight and when to parley.

From his base at Scawsby Lays near Doncaster, the Duke of Norfolk immediately began negotiations with Aske and the other leaders, promising a general pardon for all those who had been involved. Norfolk also promised the establishment of a Northern Parliament and an end to monastery closures until the so-called Northern Parliament met to discuss the matter. Aske agreed to end hostilities, not realising that he was playing right into the king's hands.

It had been a clever ploy by the king, advised as he was by Cromwell and Norfolk. Strange as it may seem Henry had the advantage of the loyalty of the rebels who were protesting against religious reforms and economic hardships. They were not rebelling directly against the monarchy, seeing the bad advice of Cromwell and others as an evil influence. Henry simply exploited their naivety.

The Archbishop of York had refused to back the rebels, objecting to a return to Papal supremacy, and as Cromwell rightly surmised further divisions soon began to spread amongst the Pilgrims. One of the strengths of the uprising had been that it encompassed all elements of society but Henry and Cromwell knew that the longer the Pilgrimage went on without resolution the more brittle and tenuous those alignments would become.

Temporising letters were sent from the king to the leaders of the Pilgrimage – but only to the leaders. In December 1536 Robert Aske and other significant figures were even invited to the king's court over Christmas. Of course, they agreed, feeling that the king really understood what they had been saying. Aske was even asked to write a history of the Pilgrimage.

Faced with what seemed to be a betrayal on the part of the more educated and well-off members of the revolt the commoners lost heart. Most of them slipped away from York and made for their farms and homes. Within a few short weeks, the mighty Pilgrim army had virtually disappeared. The Pilgrimage of Grace had been put down without even one shot being fired by Henry's troops.

In the New Year Aske and the leaders of the Pilgrimage left court and returned to their homes, well pleased by the reaction of the king and the effect of their Pilgrimage. At that point, early in 1537, Henry struck.

The Duke of Norfolk was instructed to declare martial law in the region and to administer a new Oath of Allegiance to the king. Anyone who refused to sign it was to be arrested and executed. All of the ringleaders of the Pilgrimage were taken into custody and any of the monks and nuns who had been recently restored to their houses were to be turned out. All monastic land was to be handed over to local farmers.

Henry's 'about turn' had taken everyone by surprise. Aske, more than anyone, was appalled by the king's seemingly sudden change of heart. In his naivety, he had never expected this.

Failure of the Pilgrimage was down to several factors, most notably the conflict of interests between gentlemen and commoners. Put simply, the gentlemen wanted higher rents and lower wages, the commoners wanted the opposite, lower rents and higher wages. It was, at the time, an unsolvable problem.

Aske and the other leaders were naïve and all of them misjudged the duplicity of Henry VIII and his ministers. The only possible uniting force was the church but the divide between traditional Catholic values and the new English Church was too wide to cross.

In April 1537 Robert Aske was arrested and sent to London where he was incarcerated in the Tower. He was interrogated and found guilty of treason before being returned to York. There he was hanged in chains on 12 July. The other main leaders of the Pilgrimage, over 200 of them, were also arrested, hanged or beheaded according to their station.

* * *

The failure of the Pilgrimage of Grace effectively marked the end of the road for those religious houses which remained. Some may have hung on, battling against the odds, but between 1538 and 1540 royal commissioners toured the country like a well-armed police force, obliging the remaining monasteries and convents to surrender to the king's justice.

Most of the monks obeyed the king's orders to close but those who refused, in places like Glastonbury and Colchester, were forcibly ejected. Their houses were razed and many of the monks were executed.

By the time of Henry's death in 1547 over two-thirds of all monastic lands and buildings in England had been sold off. It undoubtedly enriched the Crown but perhaps not as much as it should have done as the land and property had been sold at ridiculously low prices.

Prior to the dissolution, the total revenue for religious houses in England came to approximately £130,000 a year, over £64 billion in today's money, and once Cromwell had finished his work most of that went to the nobles who purchased the properties from the Crown. Short term gains had been the clear order of the day.

However, in January 1537, before the dust had settled on the Pilgrimage of Grace, there came a new uprising, now known as Bigod's Rebellion.

Sir Francis Bigod of Seltrington in the North Riding of Yorkshire had been involved on the fringes of the Pilgrimage of Grace. He was a known Protestant who had grown up as a ward in the house of Thomas Wolsey. Bigod saw that several of the promises made by the king to Aske and his Pilgrims had not been kept – or were ever likely to be kept.

Bigod was nothing if not a confirmed evangelist. He believed in ousting the Pope but was horrified by Henry's claims that he now had 'the cure of all souls' in his person.

Consequently, together with John Hallam, Bigod laid plans for a new rising, beginning with attacks on Hull and Scarborough. He also intended to kidnap the Duke of Norfolk while he was still in the north country and force him to negotiate with the government on behalf of the rebels.

Bigod's plot was a foolhardy plan which required the assistance of the gentry if there was to be even the faintest glimmer of success. The gentry, however, had escaped lightly after the Lincolnshire Rising and, as a group, were not inclined towards courting further trouble.

At best Bigod had only four or five hundred supporters and when, on 16 February 1517, they were beaten back from an assault on the walls of Carlisle the rising was over before it had really begun. Bigod was captured a few days later and was immediately sent south where he was imprisoned in the Tower of London.

Bigod and the other rebel leaders from the Lincolnshire Rising and the Pilgrimage of Grace were executed over the next few weeks. Bigod was hanged at Tyburn, Aske at York and Lord Hussey, the Chief Butler of England who had originally been opposed to the uprisings before changing sides, was beheaded in London. For some their end was grislier and much more horrific.

Thomas Moyne, a lawyer and one of the MPs for Lincoln, was hanged, drawn and quartered for his part in the Lincolnshire Rising. The same fate befell Sir John Barbour who had found himself involved in the Pilgrimage of Grace. His wife, however, was burned at the stake.

In all, 216 people were executed because of one or the other of the three rebellions. There seems to have been little or no distinction between the sentences and why one was condemned to a more brutal end than another remains unknown.

The three rebellions, conjoined together under the name Pilgrimage of Grace, marked the largest and potentially most dangerous moments of Henry's reign.

It was a case of 'what might have been' as, in the end, all three risings were put down quite easily. Thomas Cromwell had underestimated the reactionary element of the people when it came to their religion and the disquiet his church reforms caused to the populace remained a significant factor for the next hundred or so years.

Chapter Eleven

A Plague on All Your Houses

Eng-land in the sixteenth century – and London in particular – was a cesspool of disease and filth. The country was, quite simply, a victim-laden pandemic just waiting to happen.

It was hardly surprising. Thousands of people had migrated to England's capital city over the previous hundred or so years. As a consequence, the number of residents in the city had outgrown the available space with the result that incomers were jammed into small, badly ventilated streets and into houses with a totally inadequate supply of clean water.

Despite all this, London was perhaps the perfect barometer of the time, being particularly accurate in measuring the mood of the people. It was commonly accepted that the way in which residents of the capital reacted to laws and legislation, to military victories and defeats, was a good measure in judging the feelings of the rest of the country. If it's all right in London, community leaders thought, it will be all right in the remainder of England!

It was an accurate enough judgement but now, in hindsight, it is not always easy to see why this should be. The city was almost literally overflowing with discontent, tinder dry with enough emotion pooling in the streets to start a dozen rebellions.

Effective sewerage was almost non-existent and the River Thames which flowed through the capital served as both a toilet and a water supply for the city. People washed in muddy pools and it was not unknown for raw sewerage to come out of the communal standpipes which gave the people their only drinking water.

The cost of living was far greater in London than anywhere else in the kingdom with the result that poverty was rife. The influx of people from every corner of Britain meant that the last vestiges of feudalism, where everyone knew his place and felt relatively safe, had been abandoned. Rootless, lonely, insecure, the inhabitants of the city were far from content and were certainly not wallowing in comfort, feeding and gorging themselves on 'the roast beef of old England'.

What is clear, however, is that whatever happened in London today, the rest of England would hear about it tomorrow. News of the arrival of the plague or some other epidemic travelled fast, much faster than any good or cheerful news. And within a few days, possibly even hours of the first victim falling foul of an illness in London the rest of the country was waiting for it to appear in their parish.

All of which meant that the regular arrival of epidemics and disease was almost an expected evil. Small wonder, then, that English monarchs like Henry Tudor and his son Henry VIII built or acquired palaces for themselves, places like Richmond, Greenwich and Hampton Court, well away from the filth of London town.

Expecting it or not, if there was one thing that was guaranteed to cause disorder and fear amongst the populace it was the sudden appearance of one epidemic or another. The epidemics came, regularly, sometimes as often as every other year, one disease or another affecting everyone who came into contact with the carriers or causes.

With the diseases came anxiety and terror. Arguably, fear of epidemics like the plague was more real than any concerns the populace might have harboured about foreign invasion or rebellions. They could fight an enemy like the French or the Spanish but disease was hidden and insidious; it was something totally different.

The 'visitations' usually came in the summer when the fetid atmosphere and stench of corruption were at their height. Then panic would run wildly like the flames of a forest fire through the capital, spreading rapidly to nearby towns, villages and hamlets before moving on to more distant parts of the countryside. And there is no doubt that the population of England had many diseases to cope with in those pre-antibiotic days.

Dysentery, or 'the bloody flux' as it was known, was passed on through contaminated food or water, the sufferer being paralysed by extreme stomach cramps and diarrhoea. When the victim was left with no other waste matter to pass, blood flowed freely from the rectum. It took a strong constitution to survive dysentery.

Malaria or the ague was another ailment, particularly prevalent in the summer months. It was spread by mosquitoes which thrived in the boggy margins of the Thames and other marshy rivers. Both dysentery and malaria were common in London during Henry's reign.

Typhoid, influenza and smallpox were also regular visitors. Smallpox was known by the people as 'the red plague,' because of the rashes and puss-filled blisters it brought up on the skin of the victims. There was no cure but those who survived – by luck rather than judgement – were invariably left with scarred faces and bodies.

Tuberculosis or consumption was a constant problem, the disease being spread from one person to another mainly by coughing or sneezing. There was no known cure for TB. Once someone caught the dreaded disease it was only a matter of time before death occurred, doctors simply watching as the patient withered away in front of their eyes. TB killed Henry VII and possibly also his first son Arthur. Edward V1, son of Henry VIII, certainly died from tuberculosis, a disease that cared nothing for the position or status of its victims.

Even relatively minor ailments like gout or sexually transmitted diseases such as gonorrhoea and syphilis could be fatal as the Tudor medical profession, such as it was, had no idea how to cure them. There was no regulation of prostitutes, no health checks and almost no birth control. Adultery was common because there was little need to worry about unwanted pregnancies – after all, if the woman was married the identity of the father could always be explained away.

That did not apply to prostitutes or what were euphemistically called 'maids'. The use of sheaths offered some form of protection. Condoms made from lamb's wool were available but they were unpopular, men being far more concerned with finding their sexual pleasure where and when they could than with any form of birth control or consciousness of sexual health. Small wonder that syphilis was one of the more common ailments of medieval London.

Leprosy and scrofula were equally as common, the latter being known as the 'King's Evil' as it was said the touch of a monarch's fingers or hand could cure the sufferer. Henry IV may have died from leprosy and for many years it was claimed that Robert the Bruce of Scotland suffered from the dreadful bacterial infection that affected the skin and external body parts. Lepers were a common sight in Tudor England but they were invariably shunned, only the monks and nuns of the religious houses being prepared to offer them comfort or support.

Both Jane Seymour and Catherine Parr died from puerperal or childbed fever, a septic infection of the reproductive organs which afflicted women who had just given birth. Post-natal care was simply a case of passing the baby to a wet nurse and staying in bed for a few weeks.

Wealthy or poor, royal or religious, diseases in Tudor England and Wales were liable to attack all elements of society. Many believe that Cardinal Wolsey died from dysentery – which brought on a heart attack – while the death of Prince Arthur has been attributed to a number of different causes. The most popular theory is that tuberculosis killed him off and if we are to believe Catherine of Aragon who claimed that her nine-month marriage to Prince Arthur had not been consummated because of his ill health then that is entirely possible.

Some diseases were confined mainly to the peasant classes. Ergotism, also known as St Anthony's Fire, was one such disease that was rife during Henry's reign. Caused by eating grain contaminated by fungus (ergot), it was particularly prevalent at times when the harvests were poor and the people had no option but to eat whatever foodstuffs they could find. The symptoms of ergotism were convulsions, vertigo, hallucinations and feelings of being burned or bitten – not unlike the hallucinatory qualities of later drugs like LSD.

The two most serious epidemics or pandemics to affect England at this time, however, were the bubonic plague and the sweating sickness.

Bubonic plague had first visited Britain in 1348 and over the course of the next hundred years, the population of the country was cut by half, dropping from 5,000,000 to 2.5,000,000 million. The Black Death as it was also known, the name referring to the black buboes which soon erupted on the skin of victims, killed nearly 20,000,000 men, women and children in Europe before finally – but temporarily – burning itself out.

In its wake, the plague left devastated towns and ruined villages with the economies of whole countries being annihilated. It is all too easy to fall back on rhetoric as at this distance it is almost impossible to measure the impact the pandemic had on the population of so many different nations.

Scapegoats were required and the most obvious, certainly the most reachable, were the Jews. Christ-killers, they were called and in the wake of plague outbreaks mini-pogroms took place all over Europe. In the French city and Papal See of Avignon as many as 2,000 Jews were murdered, most of them burned alive, during one outbreak of rioting.

Inevitably, people turned to the more extreme religious sects for help. One of the most influential of these was the Flagellants who paraded through the countryside, exposing their whipped and torn bodies but offering the people an alternative to the helpless Catholic Church.

In the wake of the plague came violence and lawlessness. Theft and looting were common as houses and churches, left empty after the plague outbreaks, were easy targets. It was far from acceptable but it was understandable as those who had survived the plague seized the opportunity to give themselves some degree of comfort.

Ultimately, it was faith that got the people through, faith in a God and a system of worship that provided structure in a world that, at times, seemed to have gone mad.

After that first appearance, the plague seemed to go dormant for a while before returning every four or five years. No one knew its cause, they just had to endure it.

In fact, the plague was caused by infected fleas from black rats which, when the carrier rodents died, moved onto other available homes – in other words, human beings. In so doing they killed hundreds of citizens, particularly in overcrowded and unhygienic cities like London.

Most of the people who caught the disease eventually succumbed, survival being a matter of luck rather than judgement.

The children's nursery rhyme *Ring a Ring of Roses*, although it was sung long before the first appearance of the plague in England, sums up fairly accurately the symptoms and effects of the disease:

> Ring a ring of roses,
> A pocket full of posies,
> Atichoo, atichoo,
> We all fall down.[1]

The first line refers to the accompanying fever and red cheeks of the victim; the pockets full of flowers or herbs in the next relate to one of the few precautions surgeons could find to ward off the disease – far better than one of the other 'cures' which was to drink two glasses of urine a day! The final two lines are self-explanatory.

The first appearance of the rhyme came early in the twelfth century but when the plague appeared two hundred years later its lines and words seemed to fit the outbreak. As a result, the symptoms were quickly related to the words – not, as many think, the other way around.

The worst outbreak of plague during Henry's reign came in 1544. Henry, who was always something of a hypochondriac, immediately abandoned London, taking his court with him and heading for cleaner air and more welcoming pastures elsewhere. Behind him, thousands who did not have the same luxury of free movement had no option but to sit tight and trust to luck.

A variant of bubonic plague was the pneumonic variety. This was spread on the airwaves and infected people's lungs causing severe respiratory problems and, eventually, a merciful death. If England and the isles of Britain were smaller than the continent of Europe, the people were just as vulnerable with air-borne infections like pneumonic plague spreading rapidly and easily through what were really little more than shanty towns.

The sweating sickness was a different sort of plague altogether, appearing for the first time in the British Isles in 1485. It was said to have been brought to Wales with the invasion force and then automatically carried into England by the French mercenary soldiers Henry had employed to help him defeat Richard III.

It is possible that 1485 did see the initial appearance of the disease in Britain but that cannot be verified. What is known is that in the year of Bosworth the epidemic killed off fifteen thousand unknowing and unsuspecting citizens.

There were five more major outbreaks of sweating sickness before the last visitation in 1551, two of them in 1517 and 1528 during the reign of Henry VIII.

Once again, an outbreak of the sweating sickness in London, just like the appearance of bubonic or pneumonic plague, would send Henry into panic mode. He would immediately drop everything he was doing and head off to the country away from the filth and grime of the city. Government of the kingdom and control of national affairs were simply forgotten in the need to stay alive.

During the 1517 outbreak, Henry even cancelled Christmas. That year, he declared, there would be no celebrations, no opportunity for people to come together to make merry and enjoy singing and eating. Retire to your rooms and pray!

The origins of the disease have never yet been discovered. It struck without warning, beginning with a sudden headache and an accompanying sense of dread. These symptoms were soon superseded by shivers or tremors so violent that some of the infected victims even managed to break several ribs during this stage of the disease.

Next came neck pains and heart palpitations. Then, finally, fever, an insatiable thirst and the terrible sweating which gave the disease its name. The disease could kill within hours, many sufferers being fit and well in the morning but dead by nightfall. It was particularly ferocious and prevalent amongst the young, although babies or young children seemed to have immunity from the sickness.

There have been many theories about the cause of sweating sickness. One which might hold a grain of truth is that it was almost self-inflicted. Fastidious housekeepers would brush away the droppings of the rats which were everywhere in Tudor England and in so doing release a cloud of hantavirus-loaded dust. This was then inhaled by family members and friends with the inevitable result of infection. It is, at least, possible.[2]

In an age when superstition and belief in supernatural forces were dominant, it was all too easy for people to look at the plague and the sweating sickness as signs of displeasure from God. Visitations of these two deadly infections were, most people believed, simply punishments for failure to abide by God's laws.

* * *

Cures for any, if not all, of the terrible ailments that afflicted people during Tudor times were virtually non-existent. Survival or cure depended as much on luck as it did on skilled help.

The average life span during the first half of the sixteenth century was just thirty-five years of age; the figure was skewed by large numbers of children dying in infancy. It was one of the reasons for large families, the rationale being that many of them would die but at least a small percentage of children would survive. If you made it past childhood then there was a good chance of living until your fifties or even older.

The medical profession was in its infancy, doctors and surgeons sticking to the ancient Greek concept of the bodily humours. The world, or so the medics believed, was made up of four elements – earth, wind, fire and water Each element had a corresponding body fluid – yellow bile, black bile, phlegm and blood.

An excess of any one of these fluids could result in an imbalance in the elements and, consequently, in the personality and health of the individual. At the simplest level, an imbalance could make a person melancholic or hot-tempered. At the other extreme lay serious illness and susceptibility to ailments such as the sweating sickness.

The standard cure or treatment for almost any affliction was bleeding. This was either done by cutting into a vein of the patient or by attaching leeches to his body. There were herbal cures, as suggested by the Physicians of Mydffai in Wales. The herbal cures from this remote Welsh village and valley had helped with minor ailments for years but these had only limited success with serious diseases like the plague or sweating sickness.[3]

Purging was another treatment used by doctors. It was a simple process. The patient would be given medicine to make them vomit with the hope that the ill humours would be expelled from the body along with the medicine. Uroscopy was a standard way of discovering illness. This involved examination of a person's urine – studying its appearance, its smell, even its taste.

Put simply, the medical profession was floundering with no real idea how to help cure serious illness. There were men who gave advice – for what it was worth. Johannes Caius, physician and founder of Gonville and Caius College, Oxford, suggested that people should avoid evil mists and rotten fruit, should exercise regularly and drink herbal concoctions – shades of the Physicians of Mydffai!

Patients with the sweating sickness should, Caius advised, sweat as much as possible. The latter piece of advice now seems a little superfluous considering the fact that sweating was part and parcel of the disease.[4]

There was a belief, more folklore than anything else, that if patients could resist the temptation to fall asleep during the first twenty-four hours of going down with the sickness, they would have a decent chance of pulling through. There was little evidence to back up the claim but physicians were quick to grab and hang onto any possibility of relief.

The standard treatment for sweating sickness was to wrap the infected person in dozens of heavy blankets, ostensibly to help them sweat out the illness. In reality, of course, it was a procedure or process that was guaranteed to help induce exhaustion and weakness, meaning that the ability to remain awake was severely restricted. At some stage, usually after only a few hours, exhaustion would set in. Then sleep –and death – would come.

Cardinal Wolsey caught the sweating sickness on two occasions, managing to survive both bouts. Henry, moving swiftly from one refuge or bolt hole to the next, stayed ahead of the disease though several members of his court succumbed.

In 1528 Anne Boleyn and her father Thomas, taking refuge at Hever Castle, their home in Kent, both caught the sweating sickness. Henry was terrified and immediately sent his personal physician down to Kent to help in their treatment.

Both Anne and her father pulled through, much to Henry's relief, although there were undoubtedly many who took a different view of Anne's misfortune. Anne's brother-in-law William Carey, husband of Henry's previous mistress Mary Boleyn, was not so lucky. He died in his bed within hours of catching the disease.

Thomas Cromwell's wife and two daughters died from the sweating sickness although he himself was untouched. Cromwell's only son Gregory outlived him but died during the last outbreak of the disease in 1551.

There are those who believe that Prince Arthur's death was caused by sweating sickness. Others disagree, putting his death down to TB. There is no proof either way.

During the final appearance of the disease in 1551 both Henry Brandon, Duke of Suffolk, and his younger brother Charles died from the infection. Rich or poor, young or old, the sweating sickness, like the plague, knew no bounds. It could and it did reach out to touch everyone.

*   *   *

Bubonic and pneumonic plague affected the whole of Europe during the medieval period. Sweating sickness, on the other hand, seems to have run wild mainly in Britain.

In 1528 the English-held town and garrison of Calais suffered an outbreak but it did not spread beyond the city walls to affect the rest of France. There is no explanation for this or why the disease seems to have had a particular affection or predilection for English blood.

When the French did finally find themselves having to endure an epidemic of the sweating sickness it was as late as 1718. The French version of the disease was known as the Picardy Sweat and although it could prove fatal it was certainly not as lethal as the sweating sickness that had decimated England a hundred years before.

In 1517 and 1528 the French rather gloated at the English predicament. Considering the bad relations between the two countries and, if we believe that its origins rested with French soldiers, the lack of sympathy is at least understandable. In France the epidemic was known as the 'English Sweat'.

Like the plague, the disease was stronger and more lethal in urban environments where the great throngs of people helped pass on the sickness. Even so, there were many instances of rural areas suffering almost as badly. It was hardly surprising in a society that used communal privies and collected water from the village pump or stream. Men and women wiped their behinds with leaves or moss and then simply threw the soiled items on the ground. That certainly terrified Henry and kept him on the move, ahead of the pursuing disease.

Like most epidemics which could be passed from person to person through breath, spittle or other body fluids, sweating sickness seems to have thrived in places where there were community gatherings such as markets and fairs. Such gatherings were necessary simply for people to survive – no market, no money was the basic rule, a real Hobson's Choice for the peasantry.

The presence of large numbers of people in London for the coronations of Henry VII and Henry VIII would have also helped keep the disease active. Crowd control for such events was non-existent and all it needed was for two or three infected people to mix unknowingly with other individuals for the disease to be spread.

The peasants of England called the disease many names, the most popular being Stup-Gallant. Stup, in this context, is taken as meaning 'having a tendency towards' something; gallant is a reference to the upper elements of society. This seems to indicate that sweating sickness had a preference for the more monied classes.

Europe did not escape entirely. In 1529 there was an outbreak of sweating sickness in Hamburg, killing 1,000 people in just over a week. It then spread to Eastern Europe, Russia and Scandinavia before dying out as winter approached. Even then the sweating sickness did not affect France or the French people who seemed to have a divine degree of protection.

Although the sweating sickness is often adjudged to have originated in England and to the 1485 invasion of Henry Tudor, there must have been instances of the disease before that date.

Lord Stanley, whose neutrality until the final stages of the Battle of Bosworth Field, went some way towards helping with Henry's victory, claimed that he was suffering from the sickness as his excuse for not joining the army of Richard III. He seems to have got away with it. Richard, at least, believed the excuse if not the loyalty of Lord Stanley.

Chapter Twelve

The Exeter Conspiracy and a Bit of Rough Wooing

One of the saddest and most tragic events of Henry's reign came in the shape of the so-called Exeter Conspiracy in the year 1538. On the one hand, it was an inconsequential affair, hardly requiring the attention of the king. And yet it was a trifle that was exaggerated by Thomas Cromwell and Richard Rich in order to perfectly fit in with Henry's growing sense of paranoia and to confirm their own status within the Henrician system of government.

All of his life Henry had been haunted by the thought of a Yorkist claimant making a power grab for his throne. Real or imagined, insubstantial or powerful, the fears never left him and in 1538 it seemed to him that the paranoid vision which had so haunted him year after year was about to come true. It was a troubled and troubling time for the king, even if much of the trauma had been his own doing.

Due to the monastery closures, there had been a huge increase in the number of beggars and out-of-place monks roaming the countryside. They were a clear and present danger, a potential threat for anyone who was dissatisfied with the Tudor regime. It would have needed a titanic effort from anyone who had the mind to unite them into a 'people's army' but Henry was on edge and his mind was running riot with the possibilities of revolt and rebellion. Reality was fast disappearing over the horizon.

Logical thought had never been Henry's strong point. Now, as the end of his reign inched closer and as his fragile hold on life became ever more tenuous, he was highly susceptible to the machinations of someone like Thomas Cromwell. His ever-faithful servant would always be there for him but Cromwell had grown ever more Protestant or anti-Catholic in his religious beliefs. And sometimes those beliefs were in direct conflict with Henry's.

Henry saw this – and in his lucid moments understood it – but, surrounded as he was by men like the arch-Protestant reformer Thomas

Cranmer, not to mention Cromwell himself, the king was finding it hard to make sound, independent judgements. His paranoia could be guaranteed to kick in whenever there were 'nice' or fine decisions to be made. And Cromwell knew just how to exploit the king's weakness.

Early in 1538 letters between Henry Courtney, 1st Marquess of Exeter and Cardinal Reginald Pole, probably the most significant Yorkist still alive, were intercepted by Cromwell's agents. The correspondence apparently centred on the idea – or at least discussed it – of Courtney, who was first cousin to the king, replacing Henry as monarch after his death. It was relatively harmless but it did show the unhappiness of the country when faced with the prospect of inheriting Edward VI, a minor, as king and, therefore, the letters could be regarded as a treasonable communication.

When, in August 1538, Cromwell presented Henry with the evidence, the king immediately had Courtney arrested and sent to the Tower. It was a terrifying and perhaps bewildering fall from grace for young Courtney who, until that moment, despite his clear Catholic sympathies, had been a favourite of the king. Favourites or enemies, the distinction meant nothing to the paranoid king.

The two main reasons for Henry and Cromwell's knee jerk reaction to what were, really, insignificant letters were the changes currently being undergone in the field of religion and, more significantly, what Henry referred to as the White Rose faction. The Pole family were not only the last remnant of Yorkist rivalry – even though they had none of them, apart from Reginald, shown any inclination to rebel – but they were also a staunchly Catholic family, opposed to Henry's removal of the Pope and his own installation as head of the Church in England.

Henry could not get his hands on Reginald Pole as the Yorkist had already fled to Italy where he intended to take Holy Orders. The Pope had not waited for Pole to become a cleric but had appointed him cardinal and put him in charge of assisting with the Pilgrimage of Grace.

As it turned out helping with the Pilgrimage was an empty appointment and Pole never returned to England, as was intended. He was lucky as a return would have undoubtedly meant his capture and execution. However, by his acceptance of the role, to Henry's paranoid mind, it showed exactly where the loyalty of the Pole family lay.

Meanwhile, Henry took out his fears on those members of the Pole family that he *could* reach. Geoffrey and Henry Pole, Reginald's brothers, were arrested as was Margaret Pole, their mother, along with several other servants or minor players. The majority of those detained were incarcerated in the Tower where 'examinations' began.

Under interrogation – which is undoubtedly a euphemism for torture – Geoffrey admitted that his elder brother Henry, Baron Montague, had been in communication with both Reginald and with Henry Courtney, the Marquess of Exeter. Simply being in touch with Reginald, who from the safety of his Italian home had attempted to incite an invasion of England, was enough to warrant a charge of treason and, when backed up by the letters that Cromwell held, it was an open and shut case – at least in the eyes of the Tudor government.

Geoffrey clearly found himself in an invidious situation. To say nothing would only bring further pain on the rack or from the thumb screw and Reginald was, anyway, well out of harm's way in Rome. So why not say whatever the torturers wanted him to say? Nevertheless, despite his reasoning, Geoffrey was so troubled in spirit that in October 1538 he tried to kill himself. It was an unsuccessful attempt that succeeded only in making his captors more alert.

As a result of Geoffrey's confessions and the Cromwell letters, further arrests were inevitable. Very soon, anyone with connections to either the Pole, Courtney or Montague family was in danger of losing their liberty, maybe even their lives.

In November 1538 Sir Edward Neville, formerly the king's Chief Standard Bearer but cousin to Reginald Pole and therefore of questionable loyalty, was one of the first to be arrested. The fact that Thomas Cromwell was casting covetous eyes at some of Neville's estates was a contributing factor that was conveniently ignored.

In December Lord Montague and Geoffrey Pole joined Neville in the Tower of London. Also arrested at the same time were men who were really little more than 'bit part players' – George Croftes, John Coins and Henry Hotham. They were all put to trial and all found guilty of treason.

A few days later Lord Montague, Neville and Exeter were beheaded on Tower Hill. Croftes, Collins and Hotham, not coming from the nobility, suffered the excruciating pains of being hanged, drawn and quartered. On 2 January 1539, as a reward for his confessions which had implicated his now-dead brother and the Marquess of Exeter, Geoffrey was pardoned and allowed to go free.

Henry Pole, the son of Henry, Baron Montague, remained in the Tower and eventually just disappeared. Like the more famous Princes in the Tower before him, he was either quietly murdered or allowed to starve to death. Whichever way he died, his fate remains unknown, yet another tragedy in the story of the Tower and of the Pole family.

That left just Cardinal Reginald Pole and his mother Margaret, the Countess of Salisbury. Reginald, in his absence, was attainted by his peers and there was even an attempted assassination – a failed attempt – while he was still living and working in Rome. When Henry's daughter Mary became queen, Reginald Pole returned to England, became the last Catholic Archbishop of Canterbury and served her faithfully until his death in 1558, exactly twelve hours after Mary.

Margaret Pole was the last of the White Rose faction to suffer under Henry. She was detained first in the home of the Earl of Southampton but in November 1539 she was moved to the Tower. She was never accused or tried on any charge but on the morning of 27 May 1541, having spent over two years in captivity, she was informed that she would be executed within the hour. It would be done in a quiet corner of the Tower grounds, without fuss and without the public knowing.

Unfortunately, the chief executioner had been sent north to dispense Henry's justice in the far reaches of his kingdom and Margaret Pole was left in the hands of a young and inexperienced trainee. Whether or not a more experienced executioner would have handled things differently remains mere conjecture.

When she reached the stage set for her demise, Margaret Pole was determined not to go quietly. She refused to lay her head on the block, would not kneel before the executioner and shouted to him that if he wanted her head he would have to come and search for it.

Margaret was literally chased around the execution site by the executioner with his axe, taking swipes at her whenever he was within reach. Eventually, her head was hacked from her body and the most grisly and brutal execution in years was over.

The tragedy of the Exeter Conspiracy was that the only real evidence against either the Marquess of Exeter or any of the Pole family were a few letters that 'danced' around the question of succession.

There was also the suspect confession of Geoffrey Pole, obtained under torture, stating that Baron Montague had written to Reginald, as any man might to his brother. It was hardly a matter of great significance but in the dying days of a paranoid king, it was more than enough to signal treason and treachery.

A combination of Henry's paranoia and Cromwell's hatred of the Catholic Church had brought about what can only be described as a travesty of justice. The execution of Margaret Pole cannot be excused, either in its finality or in the sheer brutality of the event. Margaret was beatified by the Catholic Church in 1886 but it was hardly any compensation for one of the cruellest low points of Henry's reign.

*   *   *

The Carthusian Order of monks was founded in 1084 by St Bruno of Cologne. It was an enclosed order, the monks withdrawing from the world for a life of silent contemplation and prayer. They were, effectively, hermits, both monks and a small number of nuns living out their lives in solitude and seeking no connection with the world.

As representatives of a culture and belief that were beyond the understanding of most people, the Carthusian Order was attacked by the populace on a regular basis throughout the centuries. For the mobs who lurked in every city or town in Europe, they were the perfect target.

In 1419, just a few years after Martin Luther made his famous declaration at the Castle Church, Wittenberg, the Charterhouse at Cologne was burned to the ground. There were many other instances of Carthusian monks being singled out for mob violence. All of which meant that persecution was not unknown to the monks.

The first Carthusian monastery in England had come in 1181 when Henry II founded a religious Charterhouse as part of his penance for the death of Thomas Becket. Since then, a number of similar establishments had been founded.

By the time of Henry's Reformation, there were nine Carthusian monasteries in England and one in Scotland. Despite their aim of solitude and contemplation, the monks and nuns had become renowned for their charity to the poor but that did not stop Cromwell's commissioners from cutting a swathe through the Carthusian Order.

Henry had been keen to bring the monks to his side in the matter of his annulment and remarriage to Anne Boleyn. For Henry, any acknowledgement that his marriage to Catherine was illegal was well worth waiting for. The Carthusians were well thought of in the city where they were relied upon for medical aid and charity and to have them deny the authority of the Pope in favour of himself would have been a great coup.

It was not to be. The Order stood resolutely by its original position as formal members of the Catholic Church with the Pope as the figurehead and representative of God on earth. Henry was furious. If he couldn't amalgamate them into his 'brave new world', he felt that he was left with no alternative but to annihilate them.

In 1537 the London Charterhouse was dissolved by the Royal Commissioners and the monks thrown out into the streets. Trying to object and defend their house and their living, the monks fought back strenuously. In the struggle, several monks were killed and many more imprisoned. Once in captivity, they were presented with an alternative – sign their agreement to the Act of Supremacy or face the executioner's axe. They all chose the axe.

Many of the holy men were later beatified by the Pope. Three of the monks who were executed at Tyburn on 4 May 1535 – Augustine Webster, John Houghton and Robert Lawrence – were eventually canonised and became members of the forty Martyrs of England and Wales.

There were a number of separate strikes at the Carthusian Order. The first was the London Charterhouse affair of 1537 which saw Webster and the others executed. The second strike came later in the year. One of those imprisoned after the second strike was Sebastian Newdigate, a personal friend of the king. Henry even visited him in prison to offer clemency if he would only accept him as Supreme Head of the Church in England.

Newdigate, who had been kept chained in an upright position throughout his captivity, refused to acknowledge Henry as Supreme Head and was duly executed. Like all of the other 'rebel' monks, he was hanged, drawn and quartered.

A third and fourth strike effectively wiped out the Carthusian Order in England. In all, eighteen Carthusian monks were executed during the Dissolution of the Monasteries, a brutal toll on a monastic order which openly declared its intention of living a peaceful and contemplative life. To Henry that meant nothing if they would not acknowledge his position as Supreme Head of the Church in England.

* * *

As Henry neared death, by now bloated and with few redeeming features, he involved his country in yet another war with Scotland. This was known as *The Rough Wooing* and Henry was destined never to see its end. The war with Scotland broke out in November 1542 but did not reach a conclusion until March 1551 – and by then Henry VIII had been dead for over four years.

As ever in conflicts between the Scots and the English, it brought confusion and disorder to the northern counties of England, the people in the border territories being the ones who suffered most. Whatever the causes or intentions of the generals, the ordinary members of the populace were the ones who witnessed, time and time again, their land being fought over, their crops ruined and cattle killed without reason.

The Rough Wooing began when Henry attacked Scotland in an attempt to break up the Auld Alliance between the Scots and the French. There were rumours that French forces were about to use Scotland as a springboard to launch an invasion of England and that was something the English could not countenance.

Henry was also infuriated that James V, the Scottish king – son of Henry's sister Margaret and therefore his nephew – had not followed his lead and broken away from Rome. Even though he could not go public on the matter, this was an opportunity to punish James for his lack of support.

The first encounter of the war, the Battle of Solway Moss, took place on 25 November when a huge Scottish force of over 10,000 soldiers encountered an English army at least half its size.

Nominally at least, the Scots were led by Robert, Lord Maxwell, and by Oliver Sinclair but both men believed they had overall command with the result that their forces were split and the direction of the battle was at best confused, at worse disastrous.

The English under Lord Wharton and Sir William Musgrave caught the Scots on the banks of the Solway Firth and immediately launched a violent assault. Many of the Scottish soldiers were killed or driven into the river where they drowned. Over 1,000 were taken prisoner.

It was a humiliating defeat for the Scots and King James was crushed. To make matters worse, his wife had just given birth to a daughter, something which put the whole succession in doubt. Totally depressed, he died two weeks after the Battle of Solway Moss.

Henry now proposed a marriage alliance between his infant son Edward and the young daughter of James V, Mary Queen of Scots as she became known. Mary, who was to spend much of her life as a pawn, was just six days old when her father died and she was installed as Queen of Scotland. The marriage with Edward did not happen. As Adam Otterburn was to say:

> Our people do not like it and our common people do utterly mislike of it … Our nation will never agree to have an Englishman King of Scotland.[1]

The Rough Wooing continued with the added complication of a civil war raging in Scottish territory. This internal conflict between the forces of James Hamilton, Earl of Arran, and regent for Mary, the Douglas faction and the Earl of Lennox, brought considerable suffering to the people of lowland Scotland. To the very end of his reign, it seemed as if Henry would continue to inflict disorder and disharmony on his people and those of neighbouring countries.

Matters were compounded when English forces burned the town of Edinburgh. The castle on its dormant and inaccessible volcanic outcrop managed to hold out, however, but that could not stop English ships leaving Louth filled with stolen bounty and plunder.

It seemed, to the people of Edinburgh and the Lowlands, as if the sole purpose of the war had been to give riches to the English people. This needless conflict, perhaps more than any previous war ever fought between the two nations, sowed the seeds of dislike, hatred even, between Scotland and England. It was hardly the sort of requiem Henry would have wanted. A Rough Wooing indeed!

The Scottish forces fell back onto the tactics that had always served them well in the past, swift guerrilla-type raids across the border into Northumberland. More misery, death and hatred from both sides.

The Scots won the Battle of Ancrum Moor in February 1545 but then lost the Battle of Pinkie in September of the same year. With 10,000 French troops landing in Scotland, peace was eventually signed – for the time being. And so, the war, Henry's last war, continued after his death.

Nothing of significance was achieved by *The Rough Wooing* although thousands of lives, both English and Scottish, were lost. Mary, Queen of Scots, was taken to France for her safety and there she eventually married the Dauphin before finally returning to Scotland in the reign of Henry's daughter Elizabeth.

The alliance between Scotland and France continued. Henry's last fling in the war stakes had proved to be as unfulfilling as it was unsatisfactory.

Chapter Thirteen

Murder Most Foul

Like most people, the men and women of Tudor England loved a good murder mystery. And during the reign of Henry VIII, there were plenty of gruesome killings, certainly enough to catch the public interest and keep everyone guessing.

In an age without means of easy communication, gruesome stories of murder and of the deeds of murderous villains would have been spread by peddlers or, possibly, by the distribution of broadsheets. Either way, the people of distant towns and villages would have gathered eagerly in the smoky confines of the local alehouse or squatted expectantly around the fires of home to hear the news. A cold shiver up the backbone and a dread of walking alone in the dark were the obvious results of the horrifying tales.

The stories of murder rivalled even the ghost stories that all rural societies loved. They were symptomatic of the age when disruption of order was common enough but was still something to be feared and even dreaded.

One of the most bizarre cases, both in the murder itself and in the punishment meted out to the killer, was that of Richard Roose. In the spring of 1531 Roose, a cook in the employ of Bishop John Fisher, was accused of murdering two elderly residents of the bishop's house, a man and a woman who had accepted the priest's charity and were living as guests in his Lambeth home.

It was not unusual for people in distress to throw themselves on the mercy of renowned and well-off individuals like Bishop Fisher and both the man in question, Bennett Curwen, and the woman, Alyce Tryppytt, were destitute. They were obscure individuals with no connections to any religious or political enterprise but were unfortunate or unlucky in being in the wrong place at the wrong moment in time.

Roose was accused of attempting to poison, not the two eventual victims but no less a person than the host, Bishop Fisher. He did it by poisoning the soup – sometimes described as porridge – that he prepared for the evening meal.

As it happened the bishop did not eat the soup that night. In fact, he did not eat at all. He may have been fasting or may have simply decided not to partake in the meal. Either way, his refusal to take the soup saved his life. Curwen and Tryppytt were not so lucky. Almost twenty other guests at the bishop's table that evening were taken ill but managed to survive their ordeal.

After interrogation and torture, Richard Roose pleaded guilty but claimed that he had not tried to kill anyone. It was, he said, a joke that had gone wrong. He thought he was adding laxative to the soup, not poison, and was as shocked as anyone when the victims suddenly began to keel over and die. He had been given a packet of white powder, he claimed, by a stranger earlier in the day and told to add it to the soup, then sit back and watch the 'fun'. The fact that he had fled the scene of the crime only to be chased down and arrested did not exactly help Roose's case.

The court treated his excuse with disdain and he was, inevitably, found guilty. As if the crime was not enough, the punishment handed down by the court was frightening. The king himself personally addressed the Lords on the case, emphasising the seriousness of poisoning – a wholly un-English style of murder – and demanding a punishment that fitted the crime.

The Lords agreed with their sovereign and Roose was found guilty of high treason, even though his target had not been the king or his wife. Henry disliked John Fisher, who was adamantly opposed to his search for an annulment, and would probably have been happier if Roose had actually succeeded in killing him off. As it was, justice would have to be carried out and attempting to kill one of the king's bishops was as serious as attempting to kill the king himself.

The unlucky cook, it was decided, would be executed by being boiled alive! On 5 April 1531 Roose was brought to Smithfield where a huge cauldron stood ready for him. The execution was gruesome in the extreme, Roose being winched up out of the cauldron several times to ensure that the boiling water was doing its job:

He roared mighty loud, and divers' women who were big with child did feel sick at the sight of what they saw, and were carried away half dead; and other men and women did not seem frightened by the boiling alive but would prefer to see the headsman at his work.[1]

The boiling alive of Richard Roose was the only time the punishment was used in the Tudor period although it remained in the Statute Book as a deterrent for the rest of Henry's reign. The punishment of being boiled alive was removed early in the reign of his son and successor Edward.

As might be expected, rumours of the Boleyn family's involvement in the crime soon began to spread. Fisher was a major stumbling block in Anne Boleyn's route to the throne and it was widely believed that her father was the man behind the 'white powder'. Nobody offered proof but the rumour spread.

Interestingly, there was one other attempt on Bishop Fisher's life – before Henry had him executed along with Thomas More – and that involved a cannon being aimed at his house. The cannon shot caused considerable damage to surrounding buildings but failed to hit Fisher's property. As the shot had come from the direction of Thomas Boleyn's London residence the anti-Boleyn faction was quick to point the finger of blame in his direction.

* * *

Another murder – another possible murder might be a better description – which had the people of England glued to the edges of their seats for many weeks was that of Richard Hunne. Foxe, in his *Book of Martyrs*, alludes briefly to the affair:

Much about this time one Richard Hunn (sic), a merchant tailor of the city of London, was apprehended, having refused to pay the priest his fees for the funeral of a child; and being conveyed to the Lollard's Tower, in the palace of Lambeth, was there privately murdered by some of the servants of the archbishop.[2]

The death of Hunne's infant son Stephen was only the beginning of the affair which, before it had finished, caused widespread discontent and anger, most of it directed at the clergy. The problem began when Hunne refused to pay the standard mortuary fee for his dead son and found himself sued by the rector, Thomas Dryffeld.

When he attended vespers at his local church on 27 December 1512 Hunne walked into open confrontation with the priest who refused to continue the service until he had left. Pointing at Hunne he shouted 'Thou art accursed and standest accursed.' In other words, Hunne was being excommunicated by the priests and, therefore, the ecclesiastical court.

Hunne sought to use the law courts to challenge the authority of the church in the matter and in January 1513 sued the priest for slander. He would not accept any charge by a church court which was, in his opinion, the mouthpiece for a foreign body, one which had no jurisdiction in English law. The irascible Richard Hunne soon found himself arrested and sent to the ecclesiastical courts for trial on a charge of heresy.

Hunne clearly had leanings towards Protestantism and when church officials raided his house, looking for evidence, they found a copy of Tyndale's Bible in English, an illegal document in England at that time. Whether the book belonged to Hunne or had been 'planted' by the searchers will never be known.

On 4 December 1514, while still in prison and awaiting trial, Hunne was found hanged in his cell at Lollard's Tower. He was convicted of heresy after his death and on 20 December his corpse was burned at the stake. A heresy conviction after death was not unusual but burning the physical remains was certainly a convenient way of getting rid of a body that might just reveal dark secrets.

Very shortly the rumours began. Hunne had not, as was originally thought, committed suicide. He had been murdered, people began to murmur, and murdered by someone in high office. The murderer, it was said, was none other than the Chancellor to the Bishop of London, one William Horsey, assisted by two other unnamed individuals.

Furious anger exploded across London, people feeling incensed that members of the church were capable of such a crime. Mobs gathered, stones were thrown and clergymen abused. Faced with the accusation and by a growing tide of anger at the high-handed actions of the church, there was no option but to proceed against Horsey. The Chancellor chose to stand trial in the common law courts rather than the ecclesiastical one and proceedings began on 15 February 1515.

While the trial progressed Horsey was committed to prison, albeit a gaol with a fairly lenient regime. He was, the church felt, safer there until the anger had died down. And then the king intervened. Henry ordered that the case should be dismissed and Horsey set free. This was duly done but on the orders of Cardinal Wolsey, he was fined and expelled from London and not allowed to come within 150 miles of the city limits ever again. He died some years later, in abject poverty.

So, did Horsey murder Hunne? The people of London certainly thought he did and, for that matter, the king probably felt the same. Why else would he order the case to be thrown out? It remains conjecture.

* * *

Another religious murder victim was Cardinal Christopher Bainbridge who was poisoned on 14 July 1514. Bainbridge had been sent to Rome as the Ambassador of Henry VII and retained his position after Henry VIII became king. He took part in the election of a new Pope, Leo X, after the death of Julius but never set foot in his own See of York. He was made a cardinal in 1508, the year before Henry VIII came to the throne.

Bainbridge was killed by a priest with the name of Rinaldo de Moderna who had been acting as steward for the Cardinal Archbishop. His motive was, and remains, unclear. It was said that Moderna was reacting to a blow given him by Bainbridge, a notoriously violent and aggressive man. And there were also rumours that the two men were lovers who had quarrelled.

Under torture, Rinaldo de Moderna confessed that the instigator of the plot to kill Bainbridge was Silvester de Giglis, the Bishop of Worcester. He had recently become the English Ambassador in Rome and felt that the Cardinal Archbishop was a threat to him.

Giglis responded to the accusation by saying the priest was clearly mad and that nothing he said made any sort of sense. As Moderna died during interrogation it was not possible to delve deeper into the issues and no further action was taken.

The dark hand of Cardinal Wolsey might possibly be seen in the affair. With the death of Christopher Bainbridge, a new Archbishop of York was required. Wolsey had long coveted the See of York, the second most important religious appointment in England and within a few weeks of the murder, Wolsey was installed in the post. Coincidence?

Robert Pakington, a merchant and respected Justice of the Peace, achieved a degree of immortality with his murder on 13 November 1536. He was the first man in the city of London to be assassinated by a handgun.

Pakington was a friend of Thomas Cromwell and had clear Protestant leanings. He had recently expressed a number of anti-Catholic sentiments, comments that had not been well-received by the more reactionary supporters of the Catholic Church.

At 6.00am on a foggy, cold November morning he was crossing the street from his house in Cheapside to attend early service at the Mercers Church opposite. Suddenly, the quiet of the morning was shattered by a single loud bang. Neighbours and fellow worshippers jerked erect and ran to see what had happened. A group of unemployed labourers waiting, as was customary, at the Sloper's Road end of Cheapside to be taken on by some casual employer, raced towards the source of the noise.[3]

They found the body of Robert Pakington alongside the smashed lantern he had been carrying. Of his assailant, there was no sign. The use of the small wheel-lock pistol was the reason nobody saw the weapon. Unlike the large and cumbersome flintlock muskets then in common use, a pistol could be hidden under a coat or even in a pocket.

Without anyone having seen the event, finding the killer would prove impossible. A large reward was offered for information concerning the murder but the case was never solved. The crime and the circumstances surrounding it – the misty early morning, the ghostly lantern and the street empty of everyone apart from Pakington and his killer – impinged itself on the imaginations of the English public for years to come.

Thomas Trahern was murdered on 25 November 1542. As the Somerset Herald and an English officer of arms, in 1536 he had been in Scotland investigating for the Crown the events around the recent Pilgrimage of Grace.

As part of his duties, Trahern interviewed Thomas Darcy who was implicated in the rising. Darcy was later executed for his part in the Pilgrimage and Trahern returned to London where he was present at the funeral of Jane Seymour in 1537.

He was back in the north country by August 1538 when he was present at the York Assizes where Thomas Millar, the former Lancaster Herald, was condemned for his part in the Pilgrimage. The role of Thomas Trahern was obviously noted, in the convictions of both Darcy and Millar.

On 12 November 1542 the Earl of Hereford sent Trahern with messages to King James V of Scotland. On his way back from Edinburgh, near Dunbar, on 25 November he and his companion Henry Ray were ambushed and attacked by three assailants, all of whom had links to the Pilgrimage of Grace. Stabbed and run through with a lance, Trahern died quickly.

The murderers, John Prestman and the brothers William and Edward Leech, made the mistake of allowing Ray to live and he was able to identify Trahern's killers. Despite pleading for sanctuary from the church the three men were tracked down, arrested and hanged in May and June 1543. The murder of Trahern severely set back Anglo-Scottish relations, Henry blaming the Scottish king for allowing harm to befall one of his diplomats and officers of the Crown.

*   *   *

And then there were the judicial murders of the reign. There were several of these – Sir Thomas More and John Fisher to name just two – but the most significant were the killing of Anne Boleyn and of Thomas Cromwell.

There is no doubt that Anne Boleyn played Henry perfectly for the seven years between their first meeting and their eventual marriage. Whether or not you subscribe to the seven years of chastity is another matter, something that is down to individual choice.

Once the annulment of Henry's marriage to Catherine of Aragon had taken place and Anne Boleyn was installed as queen in her stead everything in the garden should have been rosy. And it was, apart from two things – the lack of a male heir and the overwhelming concept of courtly love.

Anne was pregnant when she and Henry married – which means that seven years of chastity was never a reality. Perhaps five or six? No more. Whenever Anne gave herself to the king, she miscarried that first baby and continued to miscarry. When she did give Henry a child it was another girl to match the Princess Mary.

This new princess was Elizabeth, destined to be perhaps the greatest of all Tudor monarchs. Henry didn't think so, would hardly countenance it. He wanted a male heir, in his mind the only way to keep the country safe and secure. No matter how pleased he pretended to be with the new baby girl he could not hide his disappointment and anger. A male heir was what he wanted and a male heir was what he was going to get.

If Anne had been more perceptive, she would have seen the writing on the wall. Perhaps she did but believed that Henry's love for her would keep her safe. She was wrong, both in the measuring of her husband's love and in his desire to protect her.

The second problem, courtly love, was far more insidious and yet far more dangerous, touching as it did on the very essence of Henry's manhood. The royal court had, ever since the early days of Henry Tudor, been fascinated by the Arthurian legends. Henry had even named his eldest son Arthur. A logical extension to this interest was the growing fascination with courtly love.

As a young girl, Anne Boleyn had spent several years at the French Court where she had encountered and enjoyed the concept. Deriving from the eleventh-century Troubadour poets of the Languedoc, courtly love was a way of behaving, a way of life where flirting and expressions of deep affection were commonplace:

> The sentiment of course, is love but love of a highly specialised sort, whose characteristics may be enumerated as Humility, Courtesy, Adultery and the Religion of Love.[4]

The keyword in the above quotation is 'Adultery'. Nothing physical needed to have occurred but the appearance of adultery, the idea that the individuals *would have* engaged in a sexual encounter if the situation had been different, was the important factor.

It was love on a different plane, an ethereal level where the idylls of Arthur, Launcelot and Guinevere were played out in innocent fashion. The woman was set up on a pedestal and chastely worshipped from afar, revered and obeyed, perceived as an almost religious object. During the supposed seven years of chastity that was what happened between Henry and Anne.

Afterwards, once she was married, Anne continued her flirtatious ways with her friends at court. These friends included men like Sir Henry Norris, Sir Francis Weston, Sir William Brereton and even her musician the Flemish minstrel Mark Smeaton. As Henry mithered and bemoaned another miscarriage or the lack of a male heir Anne pouted, ruled over her minions and carried on outrageously. That was what the poets and proponents of courtly love expected:

> The poet normally addresses another man's wife and the situation is so carelessly accepted that he seldom concerns himself with her husband; his real enemy is the rival.[5]

Anne Boleyn and her 'lovers' totally misjudged the effect of their behaviour on the king. They were unfortunate in that they had become embalmed in the whole concept of courtly love. That was fine if everyone believed and behaved the same but it was fundamentally dangerous if one of the parties involved was a psychotic tyrant who could only play the game so far and, more importantly, needed to play it to his own rules.

Henry watched his wife as she engaged in courtly love behaviours night after night – and he became ever angrier. He watched Norris, Smeaton and the rest, imagined them grinning about him behind their hands, smirking behind his back, and he felt like the perfect cuckold. A word in the ear of Thomas Cromwell, who was certainly not the greatest supporter of the queen, and Anne was as good as finished.

Cromwell had watched Anne's performance as often as Henry. He was no Puritan in affairs of the flesh but there had been animosity between himself and the Boleyn family for some time. Apart from anything else, Cromwell could never quite forget the part Anne had played in the fall of his mentor, Cardinal Wolsey.

When he was ready, Cromwell struck and struck hard. Mark Smeaton was arrested and, under torture, confessed to Cromwell of having slept with the queen. That was high treason and it was compounded by the evidence of other favourites like Henry Norris when they too were arrested – add in Anne's brother George Boleyn for a little incest and extra spice and the queen was beautifully fitted up.

Anne Boleyn was arrested in May 1536. She was tried before a jury of her peers, including Henry Percy, to whom she had once been betrothed, and condemned to death for adultery which was effectively a case of treason. The original sentence was burning at the stake but Henry showed some small degree of compassion and altered the punishment to beheading. On 19 May 1536 her head was taken in one stroke by the imported French executioner. A few days later Henry married Jane Seymour and, in due course, obtained his longed-for male heir.

Anne had not committed adultery, not in the accepted fashion. Her inability to produce a male successor to the throne, combined with Henry's growing passion for Jane Seymour and an inability to realise the pain that courtly love was giving to the king, sealed her fate.

All of the attributes that had made her so appealing before marriage – her sharp intelligence, her political acumen and her forwardness in giving her opinions – had proved to be not so alluring after the wedding. In the mind of Henry judicial murder was acceptable, provided it could be cloaked with necessity.

*   *   *

It is perhaps difficult to find a realistic reason for the judicial murder of Thomas Cromwell, not without falling back onto the old chestnut that he failed to provide Henry with the wife he wanted and delivered instead the upright, puritanical and totally alien Anne of Cleves. There is an element of truth in that simple schoolboy story.

For ten years Cromwell was Henry's main fixer and fabricator, the man behind the Dissolution of the Monasteries and, arguably, the evil genius behind the fall of Anne Boleyn. Nothing was too much trouble for Cromwell whose morals and trust in the service of the king were invariably questionable but, equally as certain, sure to be acting in the monarch's favour.

He had, perhaps, overplayed the attractions of Anne of Cleves, using a romanticised portrait by Hans Holbein to arouse the king's interest in this little-known princess from a tiny but thoroughly Protestant Germanic territory. On its own that was hardly enough to send him to the block but it did undoubtedly play a part.

Henry had never met Anne of Cleves until she arrived in England for the wedding and he immediately found her far too rigid and unbending for his taste. 'I like her not' was his simple declaration but by then, of course, it was too late. The wedding was arranged, the alliance with the state of Cleves forged and Henry had no option but to go ahead with the deal.

The wedding was never consummated, Henry complaining that he found no pleasure in Anne's companionship and that his new wife stank. Now, in hindsight, it seems a strange comment to make. If anybody smelled it was not Anne but Henry, a suppurating wound on his leg giving off a rancid odour that turned many a head. But then, he was king, he could say and believe what he liked.

Henry's wound was an open sore which had been obtained in a jousting accident some years before. It had never healed, the medical profession not having the knowledge or the skills to seal the wound. It constantly filled with pus and required daily attention.

Arguably, the pain and discomfort from the wound helped to advance the paranoia that afflicted the king for the second half of his reign. It certainly made him more evil-tempered than in his early days when his fuse was short but arguments and disagreements were soon forgotten. Not now, now rancour stayed and festered, not unlike the wound in the king's leg. Cromwell was one man who, more than most, often felt the vicious end of that later temper.

The real reason for Cromwell's fall from grace was the gradual slide towards all-out Protestantism which he was orchestrating. A reactionary faction at court, headed by the Duke of Norfolk and Stephen Gardiner, Bishop of Winchester, did not have too much trouble convincing Henry that his Reformation had gone too far.

Henry was a pragmatist rather than a religious extremist and, being always susceptible to the 'voice in the ear', was easily convinced that Cromwell was leading the country in a way that was both obnoxious to his beliefs and dangerous for the safety of the country.

From 1538 onwards Thomas Cromwell had led the campaign against the old religion, smashing down altars and icons in churches across the land and culminating in the destruction of the shrine for Thomas Beckett in Canterbury Cathedral. When the destruction is put to one side it remains the 1538 publication of the Great Bible, the first Bible to be printed in English, that was Thomas Cromwell's crowning achievement. Henry would not have thought so.

By 1540 Thomas Cromwell was loaded with titles and awards. He had been first elevated to the peerage with the title of Baron Cromwell of Wimbledon and was now Earl of Essex and Lord Chamberlain. He was financially secure and all-powerful but he was also ripe for a fall.

One school of thought is that Henry deliberately allowed Cromwell to achieve position and rank, thus lulling him into a sense of false security. It is possible.

Cromwell certainly failed to appreciate the strength of the reactionary element at court, undervaluing the part played by the bluff old soldier Norfolk. He also failed to see that the implementation of the Six Articles reaffirmed the traditional view of the Mass and the Sacraments.

Henry had gone along with the 'Cromwell-proposed' elements of the English Reformation, not through belief but because it had been opportune to do so. An annulment, a new marriage to a woman with whom he was besotted, enormous sums of money from the sale of monastic lands – that was where the basis of the English Reformation lay. Cromwell either could not see that or forgot it in his own fervour.

With Henry's permission, Cromwell was arrested at a Council meeting on 10 June 1540. He was deliberately humiliated by the Duke of Norfolk who tore the Order of the Garter from his body. Stunned and hardly aware of what was happening to him, he was then thrown unceremoniously into the Tower of London.

Cromwell found himself facing many charges, amongst them his support for Anabaptists. There were 'catch all' allegations such as corrupt practices and, almost unbelievably, plotting to marry Princess Mary. A Bill of Attainder was passed through Parliament and the death sentence issued. Cromwell's response was to plead – 'Most gracious Prince, I cry for mercy, mercy, mercy.'[6]

The mercy which he had, in his time, denied many was also denied to Cromwell. He was beheaded on 28 June 1540, the same day that Henry married Catherine Howard, niece to the Duke of Norfolk. By the marriage Norfolk seemed to have achieved the pinnacle of his career which had taken him from the Tower of London to the most luxurious palaces and houses in the country. He, too, was to fall from grace, thanks to the adulteries of Catherine but his fate was curiously linked to the king's and he managed to escape the block thanks to the king's death just a few hours before his own supposed meeting with destiny.

Thomas Cromwell was neither so fortunate nor so deserving. Henry was later to claim that if he regretted one thing in his life it was the execution of Cromwell but that did not stop events on Tower Hill proceeding as planned.

According to some sources Cromwell's head was cut off in one blow, in others it is said the executioner took almost thirty minutes to sever his head from his body. Either way, the head of Thomas Cromwell was displayed on a spike on the railings of London Bridge – judicial murder confirmed but a sad ending for a man who had spent most of his life giving the king exactly what he wanted.

Chapter Fourteen

The Death of a King

In his youth, Henry VIII had been a fine figure of a man, tall and handsome, well-built and with a clear-cut profile that awed anyone he ever met. His personality matched his appearance, fun-loving and open-hearted.

As he grew older, however, he also grew fatter – becoming utterly grotesque at the end – and, with the open wound in his leg that gave off a noxious odour, he was far less attractive. Far less attractive even to himself! His temper, always short, became tinder dry and by the time of his death, he was a gross parody of an over-indulged, mindless tyrant.

Henry had suffered various ailments during his life, being twice afflicted with malaria and once with smallpox. It is possible that at the end of his life he was also suffering from syphilis, one of the reasons that the wound in his leg never properly healed.

His descent into paranoia was not easy to watch and was certainly not helped by the fact that as king and lord of all he surveyed he really could make demands on people, demands that lesser men would never dream of perpetrating. He was unfortunate, perhaps unlucky, that he became king when he did.

If his brother Arthur had lived, Henry would undoubtedly have grown into a very different sort of man. To begin with, he certainly would not have become king.

He had been well-educated by renowned scholars like Erasmus and was probably the most literate man ever to take the crown. As one of his predecessors, Henry VI, found out to his cost many years before, being well-read and literate did not necessarily make for a good medieval monarch. Where that learning would have led Henry if fate had not installed him as king remains a matter of conjecture.

Never schooled in kingship, never tutored in the art of diplomacy, he had to rely on others to give him the edge in political debate and activity.

When he listened to advice he was, generally speaking, a man of good judgement and action.

One of his greatest friends and advisors, Dr William Butts, died just eighteen months before Henry. It was a sad loss for the king but at least, in his final year, he had his fool, Will Sommer, to rely on. A strange man, almost certainly someone with learning disabilities, Sommer was able to bombard Henry with 'home truths' and cloak them in the parlance of the court clown. His most famous declaration was to tell Henry that he was being duped and swindled by the fraudsters and deceivers with whom he surrounded himself. The king chose to ignore Sommer's rantings!

However, Henry's greatest failing was that he invariably came to believe he knew better than his advisors – and then, if their advice did not fit in with his ideas, he would dispense with their services. Cardinal Wolsey, Sir Thomas More and, perhaps the greatest loss of all, Thomas Cromwell all outlived their usefulness. And in the world of King Henry VIII dispensing with someone's services usually meant death.

Henry's own death was not an easy process. His last three or four years were filled with grim portents as his vigour left him and all he had to look forward to was the ultimate relief from the pain in his leg.

They were hard days and nights, filled with a continual letting of blood according to the waxing and waning of the moon and intense examination of his stools and sputum. None of it could save him and Henry knew that it was only a matter of time before he joined Anne Boleyn, Thomas Cromwell and the others in some dimly perceived and little understood nether world.

On 1 January 1547 he was stricken with a fever which many thought would spell his end. He recovered and endured the cauterising of his leg wound – painful at the best of times, agonising to a man approaching death.

Late in the evening on 27 January, Henry was asked if he would like to see and speak to anyone. He stated that he would like to exchange a few words with Dr Cranmer but that he would 'take a little sleep first' and be in a better frame of mind to talk with the Archbishop. He drifted off into a coma and never woke.

When Cranmer arrived hotfoot from Canterbury, he immediately grasped the king's hand. Knowing Henry was beyond speech Cranmer asked for a sign that he died in the faith of Christ. The king immediately wrung his fist hard and then slipped away.[1]

The king's death occurred at about 2.00am on 28 January 1547, the very day that his fallen servant and warrior the Duke of Norfolk was due to go to the block. The demise of the monarch halted all executions, Norfolk's amongst them and, according to the rules of the King's Pardon, he was allowed to live. Henry was certainly more merciful in death than he ever had been in life.

The cause of Henry's death was probably a combination of pulmonary embolism, renal and liver failure, along with the effects of obesity.

Allegedly his last words were 'Monks, monks, monks' and there were those who believed the dying man could see lines of cowled avengers waiting at the foot of his bed. True or false, his passing was not easy, not in the way his father's death had been easy.

He fought it, every inch of the way. The stench of physical decay from his wounded leg and the fuggy atmosphere of the roaring fires, lit to ward off the bitter night cold, filled the death chamber with noxious fumes. Not even the musk and other herbs used to keep the stench of death away could quite cover the smell of what was occurring.

Henry was succeeded by the little boy he had striven so hard to produce and procure. Edward VI was just nine years old when his father died, far too young to take charge of the country. Henry left him with an unfinished war against the Scots and with social discontent hovering.

That discontent was to swell into full-scale revolt and rebellion and his short reign continued to be filled with trouble and discord as his regents attempted to establish the full Protestant faith that Cromwell and Cranmer had always dreamed about.

In due course, Henry's eldest daughter, Mary, succeeded to the throne and, in a whirlwind of blood and fury brought back Catholicism to a divided country. Her reign was also mercifully short so that it was left to the unwanted daughter of Anne Boleyn to take England to the heights of political, martial and poetical glory. They were heights of which Henry would undoubtedly have approved.

It remains ironic that the world Henry VIII sought to create should be filled with discord and disharmony, both within his own reign and in those of the monarchs who followed him.

And yet, Henry's final years had been brightened somewhat by the presence of his sixth and final wife, Catherine Parr.

Catherine seemed to genuinely care for him – and he for her. Whatever sexual urges had driven the king forward in his other relationships, they had long since disappeared and the emotion which existed between the two late lovers was probably on a platonic basis.

Even the fact that Catherine was a genuine and practising Protestant did not affect their relationship. Indeed, Henry probably saved her life when the reactionary elements at court attempted to arrest and convict her of supporting the Protestant ideals of men like Martin Luther. And Catherine was genuinely upset when Henry did finally die.

It was a small comfort for the tempestuous king who, at times, seemed to thrive on discord and misery.

Selfish, opinionated, lustful and driven, Henry VIII remains the best-known of all British monarchs. He epitomises the Tudor dynasty, presenting himself to history as a lustful and mighty ruler, a man who could and would never be beaten.

He created disorder and chaos in his country, laid the foundations of the Anglican Church and began the process of changing a tiny, wind-swept island off the coast of Europe into a mighty Empire, the likes of which the world had never seen before. Changes like that had to be accompanied by disharmony and disorder.

There is no doubt that, to a large extent, the disorder reflected the character of the man. To the end of his life, Henry remained unsure about everything apart from the one desire that drove him on and, ultimately, caused the death of many – the need to procure a male heir.

Epilogue

When the people of England awoke on the morning of 28 January 1547, they did so to the sudden and certain knowledge that their world had changed. For the first time in nearly forty years, they had a new monarch.

Henry VIII was dead, of that there was no doubt. Yet, to many it seemed unreal, impossible that their larger-than-life king, a man of so many different, so many conflicting parts, should ever slip the bonds that had tied him to the earth. He was, in the words of Alison Weir:

> A legend in his own time, and under the reigns of his children, all of whom revered his memory, the legend became embedded in the national consciousness.[1]

In the centuries since the death of his last daughter Elizabeth, the final Tudor monarch, opinions about Henry – his character, his reign, his religious settlements – have changed many times. It was inevitable, given the complexities of the man and the times in which he lived.

Henry was undoubtedly a tyrant, an unbending, psychopathic monarch of limited ability and diplomatic skill – who simply did not realise his limitations. If absolute power really does corrupt absolutely, then Henry in his more manic moods was surely the most absolute ruler of all time.

At the other extreme of his character, he was cultured, well-read and appreciative of beauty in all its many forms. He remained, almost to the end, a promoter and exponent of many of the performing and literary arts.

As if all that was not enough, he was, at the same time, a bigot on a grand scale and a lover of his own voice and opinions.

Looking beyond these attributes and drawbacks, Henry was more, much more. Politically, he was a man who promoted and created, for the first time in English history, a democratic system of Parliamentary government. That fact has been largely overlooked in a welter of hyperbole over his break with Rome and the creation of the Anglican Church.

Cynics might say his reforms in government occurred simply because of lack of enterprise, intent and interest on the king's part – harsh but true, at least in part. If he began his reign by inheriting and functioning in a medieval, almost feudal kingdom, he ended it by building and shaping a modern society and state – maybe not a perfect one but certainly getting there.

Again, the cynical approach is that much of what Henry achieved was done by accident, sometimes almost as an afterthought. It hardly mattered. He was big and bold enough to cope with it. And it was a tribute to the man that his successors took and developed many of his innovations.

Like any change, political or social, Henry's achievements could only be achieved against a backdrop of disorder and disturbance. As Harry Lime remarked in *The Third Man*, the 1940s film about post-war Vienna:

In Italy for thirty years under the Borgias they had bloodshed, warfare, murder. They produced Leonardo da Vinci, Michelangelo and the Renaissance. In Switzerland they had five hundred years of brotherly love, democracy and peace. What did they produce? The cuckoo clock.[2]

Henry would surely have much preferred the Renaissance to the cuckoo clock! As long as he was remembered for something.

Throughout his reign Henry sailed blithely on, ploughing his own furrow and barely allowing his personal desires to interfere with the governing of his country. There was little doubt which one came first in his list of priorities.

There can rarely have been such a selfish British monarch, obsessed with his own personal needs and desires and, in particular, with his own fame and glory. Others would pay a price, a significant price, for that hollow accolade.

He was undoubtedly what can be termed a 'hale fellow and well met' type of man, the life and soul of the party – for an hour or so, at least. After that his personality and character would begin to irritate and even bore.

However, Henry was the king and he could irritate and bore whoever he wanted. And that was unfortunate for him and for everyone else. He should not have been king, he was never the man for the job, but he had no choice – and neither did the country.

Despite everything, after his death, the twin attributes of his fame and glory would be remembered and recalled forever. England, his England, would bask in the never-ending dream of his magnificence. He remains perhaps the most famous monarch who ever ruled this country. And that would certainly have pleased him.

Unlike his friend Sir Thomas More, who has been lauded and labelled by playwrights and film-makers with the accolade of *A Man for All Seasons*, Henry was never a man for anything more than his own brief period on the throne.

And yet he burned and blazed with a ferocity that even now lights up the sixteenth century. There really has never been anyone else quite like him. And that makes Henry VIII one of the most fascinating monarchs to ever sit on the throne of England.

Notes

Chapter One
1. Polydor Vergil, *Anglica Historia*, Book XXVII, p. 337
2. Ibid, p. 235
3. https://www.historytoday.com
4. Vergil, p. 129
5. Roger Lockyer, *Tudor and Stuart Britain*, p. 23
6. Vergil, Book XX1V, p. 131
7. Thomas Penn, *Winter King*, p. 346
8. Ibid, p. 349
9. Quoted in *English Historical Review*, Vol 127, No 524

Chapter Two
1. Polydor Vergil, *Anglica Historia*, Book XXVII, p. 257
2. Quoted in https://enwikipedia.org/wiki/Battle_of_Flodden

Chapter Three
1. Alison Grundy, *Rebellion and Disorder under the Tudors*, p. 58
2. Ibid (quoted in) p. 61
3. Lockyer, p. 42
4. Grundy, p. 50

Chapter Four
1. James Gairdner, *Letters and Papers of Henry VIII*, Vol II, p. 233
2. Commentary, *Last Letters of Sir Thomas More*, p. 141
3. Sir Thomas More, *Last Letters*, pp. 41-42
4. Commentary, *Last Letters of Sir Thomas More*, p. 188

Chapter Five
1. Alison Weir, *Henry VIII: King and Court*, p. 182
2. Grundy, Ibid, p. 60
3. https://www.ourimigrationstory.org.uk
4. Edward Hall, *Chronicles*, page not numbered
5. Ibid
6. Ibid (Quotation)
7. Edward Hall, Ibid
8. Edward Hall, quoted in www.ourimigrationstory.org.uk

9. Grundy, Ibid, pp. 52-54
10. Traditional rhyme, in *The Oxford Nursery Rhyme Book*
11. David Williams, *Modern Wales*, p. 38
12. Elizabeth Norton, *Lives of Tudor Women*, p. 153
13. Ibid, p. 132
14. David Williams, Ibid, p. 39

Chapter Six

1. Sarah Bryson, 'The Amicable Grant of 1525,' https://www.tudorsociety.com
2. Roger B Manning, *Journal of British Studies*, 1977

Chapter Seven

1. Lisa Hilton, *Queens Consort*, pp. 368-371
2. Quoted on https://www.anneboleyn.com
3. Polydor Vergil, Book XXVII, p. 337
4. Nicholas Sander, *Rise and Growth of the Anglican Schism*, p. 35
5. Quoted on https:// https://en.wikipedia.org/wiki/Witchcraft
6. Reported quote from Anne Askew, unattributed
7. Norton, Ibid, p. 225
8. Ibid, p. 156
9. John Callow, *The Last Witches of England*, p. 9

Chapter Eight

1. Ralph Griffiths, *Rhys ap Thomas and His Family*, p. 72
2. Ibid, p. 73
3. A M Sullivan, *Story of Ireland*, Chapter XXVII
4. Quoted on https://www.silkenthomas.com

Chapter Nine

1. Leviticus 18:16 and Leviticus 20:21
2. Sarah Gristwood 'Romancing the Tudors,' article in BBC History Magazine, Oct 2021
3. Quoted in Grundy, pp. 88-89
4. Ibid, p. 89
5. Ibid, p. 18

Chapter Ten

1. Susan Loughlin, *Insurrection*, p. 20
2. Ibid, p. 21
3. Quoted on https://www.tudorsociety.com
4. Quoted onhttps://www.tudor.times.com
5. Ibid

Chapter Eleven
1. Traditional rhyme, in *The Oxford Nursery Rhyme Book*
2. https://www.theconversation.com
3. Phil Carradice http://www.bbc.co.uk/blogs/waleshistory/2011/08/physicians_of_myddfai
4. https://www.wikipedia/John_ Caius

Chapter Twelve
1. Adam Otterburn, quoted on https://enwikipedia.org/wiki/Rough_Wooing

Chapter Thirteen
1. Quoted on https//www.thevintagenews.com
2. John Foxe, *Book of Martyrs*, p. 245
3. BBC History Magazine, October 2021
4. C S Lewis, *The Allegory of Love*, p. 2
5. Ibid, p. 4
6. Quoted on https:// https://en.wikipedia.org/wiki/Thomas_Cromwell

Chapter Fourteen
1. Alison Weir, Ibid, p. 50

Epitaph
1. Weir, Ibid, p. 504
2. The Third Man, film, British Lion Film Corporation, 1949

Bibliography

Primary Sources

Foxe, John, *Actes and Monuments*, aka *Foxe's Book of Martyrs*, first published 1589, republished by Hendrickson Publishers, Massachusetts, 2004

Gairdner, James, (ed), *Letters and Papers of Henry VIII, Jan–Dec 1536*, published by HMSO 1888

Griffiths, Ralph A, (ed), *Sir Rhys ap Thomas and His Family*, originally published 1620s, this edition from University of Wales Press, Cardiff, 2018

Hall, Edward, *Chronicle Covering the History of England*, Johnson Printers, London, written 1536, published 1809

More, Sir Thomas, *Last Letters of Sir Thomas More*, letters written 1534 and 1535, while in the Tower, this edition edited and published by Alvaro de Silva, W B Edmond & Co., Michigan, 2000

Sander, Thomas, *The Rise and Growth of the Anglican Schism*, published 1571, republished by Nabu Press (London) 2014

Vergil, Polydor, *Anglica Historia*, Books XXIV and XXVII, written 1512-1532, published 1534

Secondary Sources

Books

Bullock, Oliver, *The Witch Craze in Britain, Europe and North America*, Pearson, London, 2016

Callow, John, *The Last Witches of England*, Bloomsbury, London, 2021

Carey, John, (ed), *The Faber Book of Reportage*, Faber, London, 1987

Carradice, Phil, *Following in the Footsteps of Henry Tudor*, Pen and Sword, Barnsley, 2019

Bloody Mary, Pen & Sword, Barnsley, 2018

Duffy, Eamon, *Fires of Faith*, Yale, London, 2010

Gundy, Alison, *Rebellion and Disorder under the Tudors, 1485-1603*, Pearson, London, 2016

Gristwood, Sarah, *The Tudors in Love*, One Word, London, 202

Hudson, Fiona, *Weird History*, Future Publishing, Bournemouth, 2017

Lewis, C S, *The Allegory of Love*, OUP, Oxford, 1970

Loughlin, Susan, *Insurrection*, The History Press, Stroud, 2016

Lockyer, Roger, *Tudor and Stuart Britain*, Longmans, London, 1967

Norton, Elizabeth, *The Lives of Tudor Women*, Head of Zeus, London, 2016

Opie, Peter and Iona, *The Oxford Nursery Rhyme Book*, OUP, London, 1963

Penn, Thomas, *Winter King*, Penguin, London, 2012

Rees, Thomas, *The Beauties of England and Wales*, 1815, reprinted by Christopher Davies, Swansea, undated

Sullivan, A M, *The Story of Ireland*, Chapter XXXII, 1900

Weir, Alison, *Henry VIII: King and Court*, Vintage, London, 2020

Whitelock, Anna, *Mary Tudor*, Bloomsbury, London, 2010

Williams, David, *Modern Wales*, John Murray, London, 1965

Magazines/Newspapers

BBC History Magazine, June 2014, September 2021 and October 2021

BBC Wales History Blogs, 2000-2015

Journal of British Studies, Cambridge University Press, 1977

History Today, various, 2000 to date

The English Historical Review, Vol 127, No 524

Film/TV

The Third Man, Screenplay by Graham Greene, directed by Carol Reed, produced for The British Lion Film Corporation, 1949

Web Sites/Pages

https://www.ourimigrationstory.org.uk

https://en.wikipedia.org/wiki/Thomas_Cromwell

www.silkenthomas.com

https://tudortimes.co.uk

https://www.tudorsociety.com/the_Amicable_Grant

https://www.wikipedia.org/wiki/John_Caius